Lighten up, y'all

Lighten up, y'all

CLASSIC SOUTHERN RECIPES
made HEALTHY & WHOLESOME

Virginia Willis

Photography by Angie Mosier

TEN SPEED PRESS
BERKELEY

Contents

Foreword

I GREW UP IN A SMALL, rural farming town on the Florida Panhandle called Jasper, where one of the first things I learned was the importance of the family table. It was there that I learned to appreciate fresh, wholesome food, good cooking, and the fellowship of friends and family—in other words, all the things that make Southern cuisine great. Today, I have a full and fulfilling career as a chef, which gives me the opportunity to travel and cook for families all over the world—but I know that I never would have started down this path were it not for my early experiences sitting at my family's table, at home in Jasper.

The ritual of sharing a meal brings balance to our busy lives. As a chef, I have cooked for families in times of celebration and in times of great sadness. I have cooked for chiefs-of-industry and celebrities, artists and athletes—as well as people who are homeless or living in poverty. But I truly believe that when we are at the table, we are all the same. By breaking bread together, we all share in a moment of congregation and connection. And in my experience, Southern cooking is a perfect embodiment of this notion—that a shared meal is as much about *family* as it is about food.

For this reason—and many others—Southern food will always hold a dear place in my heart. But even I have to admit that somewhere along the line, Southern food became a bit of a caricature. People forgot about all those fresh ingredients, prepared thoughtfully and with love, and suddenly "Southern food" became all about butter and bacon fat, deep-frying anything that didn't move fast enough to get away, and sugar, sugar, and more sugar. The South, like many other parts of the country, became enamored with ease of prepared and fast food. Families no longer sat together at the table, started to lose their connections, and became increasingly unhealthy and overweight.

I for one have experienced these challenges firsthand. Several years ago, I was diagnosed with diabetes. I realized that I needed to make a change, to return balance to my busy life. I had fallen off track with my eating and exercise habits—it's not hard to do!—and my diabetes diagnosis was a wake-up call. I knew I had to change my diet, but I refused to change my passion for food. I have since lost over one hundred pounds, and I feel healthy and strong.

When people ask how I did it, I tell them that I just started eating the old-fashioned way. My grandfather had a large garden that produced an amazing assortment of fruits and vegetables, many of which appeared on our table as I was growing up. It was like having a farmers' market in the backyard. Our meals were centered on fresh produce; dishes were homemade and wholesome. In truth, old-fashioned Southern cuisine is perhaps the closest American equivalent to the "slow food" traditions of Europe. For me, becoming healthier and happier was just a matter of returning to the Southern food traditions that I knew from my childhood.

When I first read Virginia's book *Lighten Up, Y'all*, I felt like I'd found a kindred spirit—someone else who believes that Southern food can be healthy *and* delicious, and actually make you feel good rather than guilty. Virginia's recipes, many of which she created and refined on her own journey to health and wellness, are classic and wholesome. She encourages readers to love what they're cooking and who they're cooking for— after all, there's no better way to connect with your family and friends than by sharing a healthy and delicious meal together. *Lighten Up, Y'all* is a celebration of old food traditions, family recipes, and shared memories that I am certain you will enjoy and treasure.

by CHEF ART SMITH

Introduction

I'M GOING TO START things out talking about the F-word. No, not *that* F-word . . . I'm talking about the word *fat*. Please notice I am using the word *FAT*, which is a lot, a whole heck of a lot different than "overweight."

My entire life I have had a problem with my weight. I'm not exactly sure when it started, but photos prove I was a chubby toddler. My father was stocky, actually a boxer in the navy, and I am built a good bit like him. Which would be fine if I was a man, a boxer, or perhaps in the navy. I am big-boned with broad shoulders, and had I been a boy, I would have played offensive lineman. I am one sturdy girl, and I have most often been at least a little overweight.

Overweight is a clinical diagnosis—something a doctor would say. *Fat,* on the other hand, is the ugly word that's cruelly used in taunts on the playground or uttered in hushed whispers in junior high. *Fat* is a nagging constant in an internal dialogue about self-worth. *Fat* is the word that makes fully competent adult men and women feel like a failure.

Mama says she shouldn't have fed me so much when I was a little girl. It wasn't her fault, though—we didn't eat junk food growing up and she cooked homemade, wholesome food. Like many other Southern families, our dinners were filled with fresh, in-season vegetables, plenty of from-scratch food, and very little of the processed stuff that is so common nowadays. I just ate too much of it and, well, my genetics weren't working with me.

In high school, my insecurities about my size and weight continued. Now, when I look back and view photos of myself from my college days and even early my childhood, I see I wasn't actually fat. In fact, I was "normal"—well within the doctor-recommended weight range for someone my height. The trouble is I never felt "normal." I've only ever felt fat.

That said, food and cooking have always given me incredible joy. I was practically born in the kitchen. My grandmother, whom I called Meme, used to have a steel double sink. When I was a toddler, she would put me in one side while shelling peas in the other. The kitchen is a place of happiness for me. I don't eat for fuel; I eat for enjoyment and pleasure. Some folks overeat when they are upset. I eat when I am happy; I eat when I am sad. I eat when I am angry, joyful, depressed, elated. You name it, I will eat. I love good food.

This love of food inspired me to pursue a career in cooking. When I was twenty-five, I started to apprentice with the grande dame of Southern cooking, Nathalie Dupree. A few years later, at her suggestion I enrolled in L'Academie de Cuisine, a French culinary school then located in Bethesda, Maryland, where I learned techniques for making pâtés and terrines, soufflés, the five French mother sauces, and bread and pastry. Of course, I also learned about the most iconic French ingredients of all: butter, butter, and more butter. I actually witnessed a chef deep-fry *bâtonnets* of butter coated with a mixture of bread crumbs and herbs to serve with steamed asparagus. (*Fried butter*, you say? Well, it was absolutely delicious.) Ironically, I was the thinnest I had ever been in my life. I was actually skinny. Yes, I was eating rich foods then, but not the junk food or processed food that I sometimes ate in college because they were so convenient. I was walking several miles a day both to culinary school and to work at a restaurant; I had a healthy lifestyle.

Later, I moved to France to learn more about French cooking. At École de Cuisine La Varenne, at Château du Feÿ in Burgundy, I made quiche with triple-cream cheeses that were heady and dense with the flavors of the pasture; served platters laden with spicy, meaty saucisson that was nearly primal with animal essence; and prepared delicate, flaky, tender pastries that seemed to consist of layers of buttery air and flour.

But my formal culinary education didn't teach me *everything* I know about cooking. After all, I come from a long line of ladies who know their way around a kitchen. My grandmother was renowned for her buttermilk biscuits, fried chicken, macaroni and cheese, apple hand pies, and blackberry cobbler. My mother loves to bake, and her pecan pie, angel food cake, and pound cakes are legendary. It's not surprising that my family is full of good cooks; after all, food is central to the South's personality and character. We define ourselves and our lives by the food in our kitchens and the food on our tables. And what I love most about Southern food is its diversity: it is truly a mixture of *many* wonderful regional traditions, with Native American, European, and African roots. There's the Low Country cooking of the Atlantic coast, which showcases rice and seafood; Deep South cooking that relies on corn and products made from it, such as grits, cornmeal, and hominy; the mountain cooking of Appalachia that features food foraged from the land and rivers; French and Spanish influences on the Creole cuisine of Louisiana and the Gulf Coast.

In other words, Southern cooking is about more than just fried chicken and fatback. To say otherwise would be the same as saying Chinese food is just eggrolls or Italian food is just spaghetti. In fact, traditionally, Southern cooking was a vegetable-based cuisine. In most of the South, the growing season is almost twelve months long. This is the fertile land of okra, green beans, tomatoes, and corn. Southerners didn't eat this way solely for health reasons, not at all. For the most part, the plant-based diet was a symptom of the poverty that affected the entire South, both black and white—eating a lot of meat was simply too expensive. In fact, that bit of pork in the greens might have been the only

meat in the pot. Many Southerners grew their own food, and when they did eat meat, it was often raised on the farm or wild game or seafood culled from the forests, rivers, and sea.

So, what lessons can we learn from the way our parents and grandparents used to eat, and from the origins of Southern cuisine? Eating in moderation and relying mostly on plant-based cooking is certainly one of them. I love fried chicken and fatback, but I don't eat them all the time. I also like starting the day with a steaming hot bowl of stone-ground grits topped with sunny-side up farm eggs and country ham, crowned with a homemade biscuit. But I can't eat that way every day and no one should. You say, "My grandpa used to eat biscuits with sausage gravy every morning for breakfast, and he lived to be 100!" Well, maybe. But I'll bet you don't wake up at 4 a.m. to plow the field, milk the cows, or work the farm like he did. In other words, we're not working hard labor all day to counteract the calories.

Another thing that has changed since our grandparents' time is the ubiquity of processed, prefab meals. Forty years ago you could get a tender, flaky homemade biscuit to go with a fried chicken dinner at any number of meat and threes all across the South. Today, most casual dining restaurants use a boxed mix or frozen biscuits. Cakes and pies are made from mixes that are as much flour as chemicals and preservatives. They are baked, boxed, and shipped from a central commissary to arrive on shelves where they seemingly never age or spoil. Even our iconic iced sweet tea has been replaced with a bottomless Big Gulp of soda. What happened to real Southern cooking for real people? Well, convenience is what happened. Somewhere along the line we lost our way in the home kitchen on the way to the drive-through.

Economic factors certainly contributed the South's obesity epidemic, too. Fresh produce and organic, wholesome ingredients can be expensive, and if you're on a limited income, then you're obviously going to buy cheap food. Here's where fast food enters the equation—and cheap food (fast or otherwise). Foods that are cheap tend to have a lot of sugar, salt, and fat. According to a survey by the Centers for Disease Control released in 2012, at least 30 percent of adults were obese in thirteen states: Alabama, Arkansas, Indiana, Iowa, Kentucky, Louisiana, Michigan, Mississippi, Ohio, Oklahoma, South Carolina, Tennessee, and West Virginia. It's not surprising that many of these states—especially the Southern ones—also have some of the highest poverty rates in the nation.

So, yes, it's true that statistically speaking, Southerners are at risk for being overweight and unhealthy. But I do not think that we should let statistics govern our lives, and I definitely don't think that the risk factors should allow us to just give up on living a healthy lifestyle. I also know how dangerous it is to fall back on stereotypes about the Southern diet, even if there *has* been a proliferation in the media and on television of unhealthy Southern cooking. Let me tell you, I have never had a bacon-wrapped, deep-fried macaroni and cheese square or a hamburger on a donut bun in my entire life. My Southern grandmother, who ate a lot of fried chicken and fatback—and lived to be ninety-two—would have been absolutely appalled.

As a Southerner who has struggled with weight for much of my life, I felt like I needed to take a stand, make a change. I knew that it was possible to cook healthy Southern food—I'd seen my family do it for generations—and I wanted to share that knowledge with others. I also wanted to quell the voices in my head. I joined Weight Watchers and lost forty pounds. It absolutely changed my life. My life continues to change. My cholesterol and glucose levels are great. I exercise at least five days a week and I feel really good. I am strong and healthy. I am happy. Is this a lifelong journey? Yes. Will I continue to have to watch what I eat and exercise? Yes. Do I still love food? Yes—a big, loud, resounding YES!

I know firsthand how crippling the F word can be to self-esteem. But, this is not a book about saying "no." This is a book about saying "yes!" This book is about what you *can* have, not what you can't. This book is about real food and clean eating. This book is about food that tastes good. It's packed with tips and techniques for sensible eating and ways to succeed. Each recipe has the nutritional information you need to make good decisions. This is not a diet book. I'm not a nutritionist, dietician, or a doctor. I am a French-trained Southern chef.

How did I go about choosing which recipes to include in this book? The first and most important criterion was that *it had to taste delicious.* I wanted to showcase my favorite recipes—classic Southern dishes that I grew up eating, or cooked as a professional chef—but make them lighter, lower in fat and calories, and higher in fiber than their more traditional counterparts. Since the keys to healthier eating are balance and moderation—not denial—I've tried to include recipes for every occasion, be it an easy weeknight dinner or a celebratory Sunday brunch. Every aspect of the meal is covered, from starters and nibbles to memorable side dishes, main courses, and yes, sweet indulgences, because no book remotely Southern would fail to pay homage to the Southern sweet tooth!

Who doesn't love a good Southern-style feast? Piping hot smothered chicken and gravy, collard greens with potlikker, bubbling macaroni and cheese, skillet vegetable cornbread, and fruit cobbler? Southern food is comfort food and everyone has a favorite dish that takes you immediately back to your childhood. It's true that "comfort food" often means "notoriously high in calories and saturated fat"—but it doesn't have to! I've found a way to lighten even the most "comforting" dishes out there.

This book lightens America's favorite Southern recipes to make them a better choice for good health, while keeping the traditional flavors intact. After all, at the end of the day I'm still a classically trained chef who loves to eat, so if a healthy variation doesn't taste as good or authentic as the original, well, it didn't make the cut.

Lighten Up, Y'all is not a diet; it's a way of life. More than that, it's a totally doable, truly enjoyable way of life that will allow families across America to enjoy delicious comfort food and still stay healthy. If you've read my previous cookbooks, *Bon Appétit, Y'all* and *Basic to Brilliant, Y'all*, I think you'll have fun with my new cooking approach. And if you're a newcomer, welcome to you, too! There's a world of healthy Southern flavor waiting for you if you turn the page. Welcome, once again to my Southern kitchen. Pull up a chair.

Bon Appétit,
Y'all!
Virginia Willis

NUTRITIONAL INFORMATION

You'll note that the recipes in this book all include nutritional information. I partnered with Anne Cain, an experienced food editor and award-winning dietitian, to calculate the calories, fat, carbohydrates, fiber, and protein for each recipe. Each main recipe is analyzed by serving, and sauces and condiments by tablespoon.

I've also included nutritional information that will help you make good decisions about your eating habits. You will see many recipes that are low in calories, fat, and carbohydrates, but high in fiber and moderate in protein. At the end of the day, weight control is all about calories in and calories out. Eating to fall below or to meet your daily recommended allotment of calories will result in weight loss or weight maintenance. And increasing your physical activity, from running on the track to running the vacuum, will aid you in your weight loss or weight management. In practical terms, that means that if I am hungry, I start my meal with a heaping helping of broccoli, which I love, and have a smaller portion of protein. It's a livable method that doesn't make me feel deprived, and I feel rewarded on multiple levels when I exercise!

More in-depth nutritional analysis includes sodium, percentages of daily values, and other considerations. That's not what this book is about. This book is about helping you make tasty and healthy choices. When you review the nutritional information, please know that it refers to the primary recipe listed and *not* the variations. So, for example, if a dip is served with an endive leaf as the first choice and cracker as the second, the nutritional information is only in regard to the endive leaf.

TOOLS FOR THE HEALTHY SOUTHERN KITCHEN

While I am not a gadget guru, I do feel there are certain kitchen tools you need at your disposal for cooking, even more so when you are trying to lighten things up. It's true, from-scratch cooking can take a bit more time. And I've found that even the smallest impediment might cause you to make a poor decision, or to just give up completely! For example, oil can be used to keep things from sticking to a baking sheet—but so can a nonstick silicone baking mat. Having a scale right there on the counter makes it easy to weigh your proteins so that you don't accidentally overeat. It's not one big thing that will lead to your success; it's lots of little things.

A decent set of both liquid and dry measuring cups is absolutely mandatory. Liquid and dry measuring cups hold the same volume, but they are specifically designed to accurately measure their respective ingredients.

I suggest two sizes of liquid measuring cups: a 4-cup measure for mixing sauces and such and a 2-cup measure for smaller amounts. Liquid measuring cups have fill lines below the rim and a spout so they are best for pouring. (While you could fill a dry measuring cup with liquid to the brim you're very likely to spill some before it gets into your recipe.)

For measuring dry ingredients, you need a good set of dry measuring cups. To use them, the best method is to scoop and scrape: fill the cup with flour, for example, then using a flat edge like the back of a knife or a rubber spatula, scrape across the top to remove the excess. It's not advisable to measure dry ingredients in a liquid measuring cups because you can't scoop and scrape.

I'm a professional recipe developer, and yes, even I measure as I cook and portion my food. It's incredibly important when I want to accurately judge how much food I am eating down to the very last spoonful. Get a sturdy set of measuring spoons and keep them at the ready.

There's no need to spend a fortune, but you will need an accurate digital scale if you want to measure your portion sizes correctly. (You can buy a reliable one for less than thirty dollars online.) Sure, we all know about the visual aids for gauging portion size—like 3 ounces of meat is about the size of a deck of cards and 1 cup of rice or pasta is the size of a tennis ball, but a scale eliminates the guesswork. (A 1½-ounce portion of cheese is the size of three dice. Okay . . . but how big is that? I can't remember the last time I rolled dice.) I always leave my kitchen scale on the countertop so it's right there when I need it. Out of sight can mean out of mind.

I also keep a squirt bottle by my stovetop filled with canola oil. I know that three squirts of my particular bottle is one teaspoon. I also have a selection of silicone brushes to help move that teaspoon's worth around to coat the entire bottom of the pan with just a whisper of oil. I use this when searing meat and fish. I've gotten in the habit of using nonstick spray for ingredients like vegetables, since a quick spray coats the bottom of the pan and is only a few calories. You'll be amazed how little oil you actually need to cook—and how easy it is to be heavy-handed and pour out too much if you're going straight from the bottle.

Nonstick skillets work. I'm on record as not being a big fan because they don't readily allow for the creation of fond, the delicious brown bits of goodness that develop on the bottom of the pan when searing meat that are indispensable in a pan sauce. In the past, I thought they were best for cooking eggs and pancakes. But now that I watch what I eat more carefully, I see the light. A nonstick skillet requires far less oil than a stainless steel skillet. When using a nonstick pan, never use metal utensils to stir food because you can nick and scrape the surface. Use wooden or silicone utensils instead. The alternative is a *very* well seasoned cast-iron skillet. My grandmother's skillet is still my go-to piece of cookware. Don't think I don't see the irony of cooking lightened up Southern food in a 100-year old skillet that's likely fried an entire chicken house of hens.

Nonstick silicone baking mats are indispensable. They are superb for roasting vegetables with just a little oil like with the Delicata Squash Chips (page 17). I will often slice a head of cauliflower or a chop a head of broccoli into florets and simply roast them on a nonstick baking sheet with a bit a salt and pepper—maybe a dusting of curry on the cauliflower—and a quick mist of nonstick spray. Those are almost "nonrecipes," and practically calorie free. The mats are great for cooking cutlets and burgers and perfect for baking the sensible cookie splurge. While you can use a parchment-lined baking sheet, the silicone baking mats allow for a bit of sizzle on the baking sheet and won't become a soggy mess. They are reusable, nearly indestructible, and greener than using parchment paper because you can wash and reuse them.

I recommend buying several solid metal oven-proof cooling racks that fit snuggly into your baking sheet. I've seen them sold in a three-pack at Costco, and you can also get them at your local cookware store. I often roast meats and vegetables on them, rather than directly on the baking sheet, since the rack helps air circulate all around the food to get it nice and crisp. It also allows the fat and oil from cooked meats to drip onto the baking sheet and not wind up on your plate.

THE REAL SKINNY ON FATS

Fat definitely gets a bad rap—and there's a lot of conflicting information about "good" fats and "bad" fats, and if and how you should incorporate them in your diet. There is a well-established link between fat intake and the risk of heart disease and stroke. And according to the American Heart Association, diets that are overly rich in "bad fats"—saturated fat and trans fat—cause high LDL cholesterol (the "bad" kind that your doctor tells you to avoid).

But, as with all things, moderation is key. No-fat and low fat aren't always the best strategy. According to the Harvard School of Public Heath, low-fat processed foods are often higher in sugar, carbohydrates, or salt than their full-fat counter-parts. Diets high in heavily processed carbohy-drates can lead to weight gain and an increased risk of type 2 diabetes and heart disease. And, for good health, the type of fat matters more than amount. Remember, losing weight is all about cal-ories in and calories out—not just no-fat, low-fat, or no-carb and low-carb.

Cooking Fats for the Healthy Southern Kitchen

So the big question is, what's the best way to use fat smartly in your cooking? Sometimes this can be a bit overwhelming and it was challeng-ing for me—a trained chef!—to learn. Elements to consider when choosing oil include flavor and smoke point. In terms of flavor, choosing which oil depends on what will taste best in your dish; some have robust flavor while others don't have any. The smoke point of cooking oil is just what it sounds like: the temperature at which the oil will start to smoke—just before it completely degrades and catches on fire! When oil gets too hot, it loses its nutritive value, turns dark in color, starts to smell like bug spray, and tastes pretty bad, too. So, if you see wisps of smoke coming from the oil in your skillet, it's time to take it off the heat, toss it out, and start with fresh oil.

CANOLA OIL is among the healthiest of cooking oils. It's high in omega-3s, a class of unsaturated fat that helps promote healthy blood circulation and reduce inflammation. There are claims that canola is poison, GMO, causes Mad Cow Disease, you name it. The USDA disagrees and I do as well. Canola oil comes from the canola plant, a genetic variation of rapeseed. (Rapeseed oil is an industrial oil, and canola was developed using traditional plant-breeding methods to make the rapeseed edible.) As a chef, I often use canola oil because it's flavorless and allows the flavor of the food shine through. Most canola in the United States is genetically engineered, so I choose to buy organic, which is not. I also buy expeller-pressed canola oil, oil extracted by a chemical-free mechanical process. Canola is a good all-purpose cooking oil and is excellent for sautéing, frying, and baking, or for use straight from the bottle for salad dressings, mayonnaise, and vinaigrettes. I prefer to use organic canola spray for a nonstick cooking spray. It has very little flavor, high smoke point for high heat cooking, and no aftertaste, which some of the other cooking sprays seem to have. It's hands down my favorite oil in the kitchen.

OLIVE OIL is at the heart of all Mediterranean cooking. Extra-virgin olive oil is cold-pressed and is the least refined of the olive oils. Cold-pressing aids in preserving and retaining various vitamins and nutrients. Depending on the olives from which they were pressed, olive oils will vary in flavor and aroma. This oil is best for cooking over low to medium heat, due to its low smoke point. The finest extra-virgin olive oil is best used as a finishing touch on a dish rather than for cooking. Pure olive oil is slightly more refined than extra-virgin olive oil and has a higher smoke point. It is best for sautéing at medium heat. Both oils are flavorful and best used where the oil's full flavor is intended as an integral part of the finished dish.

SAFFLOWER AND SUNFLOWER OIL These oils are both used as cooking oils in cuisines over world. Produced from related flowers, they are very versatile. Safflower oil is a favorite for salads because it doesn't solidify when refrigerated and chilled. Both can be used in cold dressings and mayonnaise as well as high-heat cooking and sautéing and are neutral enough for baking. These oils are heart healthy and fairly inexpensive.

VEGETABLE OIL Growing up, my grandmother had a small bottle of "salad oil" in her cupboard. That's a pretty nondefinitive term, much like "vegetable oil." It's a bit sneaky; for the most part, vegetable oil is actually soybean oil with a few other plant-based oils blended in. Since the combination varies, it's more challenging to determine its health benefits, if any. The deal with vegetable oil is that it's less expensive than pricier oils such as olive, sunflower, or safflower. Vegetable oil is widely available and can be used interchangeably with other oils.

BUTTER Classic French cooking pretty much considers butter to be a food group. My view on butter is that, if you're going to eat it, you may as well eat the absolute best since the highest-quality butters have the same amount of calories as the cheap stuff. The great part is that just a little butter will go a long way. Butter lends a smooth and creamy taste to foods and is silky on the mouth and tongue.

Fat 101

Equal quantities of all fats have about equal calories. In regard to weight loss, all fats should be used in moderation. As a cook, I decide which fat to use in terms of flavor, the cooking method, and health benefits.

UNSATURATED FATS are found mainly in many fish, nuts, seeds, and oils from plants. These fats may help lower your blood cholesterol level when you use them in place of saturated and trans fats. Foods containing unsaturated fat include salmon, trout, herring, avocados, olives, walnuts, and vegetable oils such as soybean, corn, safflower, canola, olive, and sunflower.

Omega-3 fatty acids are class of unsaturated fat. They are found in foods including walnuts, some fruits and vegetables, and coldwater fish such as salmon, herring, mackerel, sturgeon, and anchovies. Omega-3 promotes healthy blood circulation and helps reduce inflammation. The bottom line on unsaturated fats is that these are the ones you want to use the most.

SATURATED FAT is found mostly in foods from animals and some plants, including coconut, coconut oil, palm oil, palm kernel oil, and cocoa butter. Too much saturated fat can raise cholesterol. The bottom line on saturated fat is that they should be used in moderation.

TRANS FATS OR TRANS-FATTY ACIDS are mainly found in processed hydrogenated oils such as margarine and shortening and processed foods made from processed oils. They are also found in lesser amounts in animal products such as beef, pork, lamb, butter, and milk. Some science indicates naturally occurring trans fats aren't as harmful as those that are from processed foods. Companies like using processed trans fats in their foods because they're cheap. Stay away from processed foods with trans fats.

TEN TIPS FOR LIGHTENING THINGS UP

I believe in the concept of "kaizen," the Japanese business philosophy of continuous improvement of working practices and personal efficiency. It's as simple as "Do what you can when you can—it doesn't have to be all or nothing." Daily improvements are as simple as one small movement forward at a time. Try to incorporate some of the tips below in your everyday life; a little goes a long way.

1. **DRINK UP**. Start every meal with a glass of water. Think you're hungry? Drink a glass of water. Craving a snack so bad you can't stand it? Drink a glass of water. It's easy for your body to mix up hunger and thirstiness, and sometimes, all you really need is some water to satisfy your pangs. At a party and want a glass of wine? Have a glass of water. If you throw an occasional glass of water into the mix, you'll find that you've drunk less wine at the end of the night. Sure, sometimes you will go ahead and have that snack or glass of wine after a glass of water—but at least it will be a thoughtful choice, not just a knee-jerk reaction.

2. **EAT MORE, NOT LESS!** Forget diet denial and being hungry. That's a surefire way to set yourself up for failure. It makes me grumpy; I call it "hangry." Worse yet, if you deny yourself over the course of the day, you're more likely to overeat the next time you sit down for a meal. If you feel hungry, don't ignore it—reach for some vegetables or fruit.

3. **CHOOSE LEAN PROTEINS**. We all know that salads are healthy—and they can be tasty, too. But there's nothing worse than eating a big green salad and then feeling hungry again an hour later. If you're trying to lose weight but eating foods that leave you unsatisfied, you're going to start prowling the cupboards. Augment your meals with some lean protein, which helps keep you full and more energized for longer.

4. **SPICE IT UP**. Boldly flavored foods stimulate your taste buds, leaving you more satisfied. The result? You won't eat as much. So say "no" to bland food and instead, bump up the spice and seasonings. You'll notice a lot of smoked paprika and other savory flavors throughout this book.

5. **GET OFF TO A GOOD START**. Breakfast is important. You might think you are saving calories by skipping, but eating breakfast actually kickstarts your metabolism for the day. Eating a healthy meal soon after waking means you're less likely to pig out later in the day.

6. **BE MINDFUL** Put down your smartphone and turn off the TV. When you eat, you need to sit down at a table and be mindful of what you are eating. Think about it. Notice the texture, the aroma, the sounds of what you are eating. If you pay attention instead of just eating, you will realize when you actually get full.

7. **VEG FIRST**. We're accustomed to making a bed of pasta, rice, or potatoes and then putting the meat and vegetables on top—but that's a lot of carbs. Instead of putting vegetables on top of a pile of rice, put the rice on top of a pile of vegetables. Vegetables should occupy the largest amount of physical space on your plate.

8. **MEASURE UP**. Measure when you are cooking and serving your plate. Don't eat from the bag; measure out chips, nuts, and other snacks.

9. **EAT DINNER EARLY**. Our natural metabolism dips while we are sleeping. Longer lapses between large meals allow your body to process food more efficiently. So, although during the waking hours it's good to feed yourself little meals every few hours, during sleep it's best to let your body have time to metabolize the food. There's something to the expression "Eat breakfast like a king, lunch like a prince, and dinner like a pauper." Think of food as fuel for what's *about to happen*, not what's already happened. You don't need as much fuel for when you are resting. And, eating late is tougher on your willpower and can tend to make you eat more.

10. **MAKE IT A PLAY DATE**. Instead of going out to eat or hanging at happy hour with friends, make a play date. Connect for a walk at a park, schedule some time to volunteer together, visit an art studio, or sign up for a ceramics class.

CHAPTER 1

STARTERS

and

NIBBLES

LET'S GET THIS PARTY STARTED! How do Sinless Seven-Layer Dip, Barbecue Meatballs, and Grilled Shrimp and Pepper Poppers sound to you? If you're anything like me, you're probably thinking, "Virginia, of course that sounds delicious, but I can't eat that and be healthy!"

Well, the good news is, I've found a way to make starters—which despite their small size are often loaded with fat and calories—both healthy *and* tasty. Because let's face it: appetizers bring the party. Whether they're served as a meal starter, or tapas-style small plates, as the main event, appetizers are fun, festive, and one of the most enjoyable parts of entertaining. (Not to mention how nice it is to start an any-night meal at home with a little nosh or nibble.)

Standard fare at a game day party might include deep-fried Buffalo wings, chips and salsa, and spinach dip. Cocktail gatherings often liberate legions of premade quiches from the cold case at the big box store. Busy hosts start dinner parties with a selection of cheeses and charcuterie platters. Supper clubs give gourmets a chance to strut

their stuff. Yikes! That's pretty hard temptation to stand up to. And face it, raw broccoli florets and dry, air-popped popcorn just don't cut it.

But my motto is that healthy eating is all about making good choices, not "no choices." So let's rethink this. What can we serve that tastes wonderful, is good for you, and will make your guests smile?

How about Delicata Squash Chips, Cornmeal-Crusted Chicken Bites, and Slice-and-Bake Parmesan-Herb Cheese Straws? Of course the standard vegetable platter is a good idea. But even better would be to make it special: if you pick up premade crudités at the store, take a moment to lightly cook the broccoli and freshen up the celery and carrots in a bowl of cold ice water. I think that a vegetable platter is only as good as its dips, so be sure to have a selection of healthy choices nearby. In the summer, set out some Smoky Eggplant Dip, Lightened-Up Pimiento Cheese, and even the Jalapeño Dipping Sauce for the Cornmeal-Crusted Chicken Bites with Belgian endive leaves and butter lettuce for dipping and wrapping. In autumn and winter, serve butternut squash puree (which is low in calories, fat, and carbohydrates) with crispy lardons of country ham; or sliced pear with crumbles of bold, flavorful blue cheese—just enough to accent the squash. And while we're on the subject of vegetables, don't forget pickles: there are so many different varieties available at farmers' markets and grocery stores, literally from asparagus to zucchini, and they're all deliciously healthy.

If this all sounds like a lot of work, remember, it doesn't *all* have to be homemade—just think a bit outside the (cream cheese) box. Kids and adults alike love edamame in the pod. Nuts—which are a party staple but also packed with calories—aren't off the table, but they do need to be in the shell.

You will eat less and more slowly if you have to crack them to eat them. Seafood, while often a bit more costly, is a great, healthy choice for starters and nibbles for both fetes and family fare. Maybe looking for a little splurge on Wednesday night to celebrate a good day at work? Shrimp, smoked trout or salmon, and oysters are spectacular—they're low in calories and fat, but high in protein, which makes them very filling.

The recipes in this chapter are certain to become favorites for parties at home and potlucks with friends. Everyone loves a good party and you're going to love these starters and nibbles whether you're trying to lighten things up or not. Forget counting calories—this food is just flat out good!

BOTTOMS UP

If you are watching what you eat and not what you drink at a party, you might find yourself in dangerous territory. First, you'll find that the more you drink, the easier it is to, well, *slip* when it comes to healthful eating. Second, alcohol is considered "empty calories," meaning, there's no nutritional value, only calories. As a good Southern girl, I like a bourbon, and as a French-trained chef, I love wine, but the fact is that 5 ounces is still around 125 calories and a mere 1¹⁄₂ ounces of hard liquor such as bourbon is 100 calories—that's hardly enough to wet your ice cubes. As I mentioned in my ten tips (page 12), drinking water will help keep you in line—you won't keep reaching for a drink refill, and your stomach will feel full more quickly, so you don't eat as much. As always, exercise is a good idea: when I am going to a party, I make sure I exercise a bit extra and plan for it with the menu choices I make that day.

DELICATA SQUASH CHIPS

MAKES ABOUT 50 PIECES TO SERVE 5

These are as addictive as any potato chip; I guarantee it! I will often bake them to nibble on while I am making dinner, since I like to nosh while I cook. As you can see in the photo, I prefer to thinly slice the squash into rings, seeds and all. It can be a bit tricky to slice the round squash on a flat surface. A more cautious approach is to first halve the squash lengthwise. (For more tips on how to slice hard vegetables, see the note on page 176.) Then, once you have a flat surface, you can choose to remove the seeds or not. To remove them, scrape the seeds out with a teaspoon, then cut the squash into thin half-moons instead of rings.

1 delicata squash, ends trimmed

Organic nonstick cooking spray

Coarse kosher salt and freshly ground black pepper

Calories 30
Fat .6 g
Carbs 7 g
Fiber 1 g
Protein .6 g

Preheat the oven to 350°F. Line two rimmed baking sheets with silicone mats or parchment paper. Using a chef's knife, thinly slice the squash into $1/8$-inch-thick slices. Place the squash without crowding on the prepared baking sheets and lightly coat with cooking spray. Season with salt and pepper. Transfer to the oven and bake until crisp and lightly charred, about 25 minutes. Serve immediately.

SINLESS SEVEN-LAYER DIP

MAKES 6 CUPS TO SERVE 24

Seven-layer dip is one of those decadent, delicious dips that render folks absolutely senseless, so before you know it, you find your willpower has gone way south of the border. Don't tell anyone this is a healthier version, and I promise they will never know. I learned the technique of extending the creamy avocado in the guacamole by adding steamed broccoli, peas, or edamame at Rancho la Puerta, in Tecate, Mexico, a destination spa where I teach Southern Comfort Spa Style. It's a great tip to use as a layer in this dip, or just when you make guacamole solo.

Try this with the delicata chips (page 17) and let's go skinny-dipping.

1 (14.5-ounce) can low-sodium pinto beans, rinsed and drained

1 teaspoon ground dried red chiles

Juice of 1 lime

1 avocado, halved and pitted (see note, page 41)

1/2 cup broccoli florets, shelled English peas, or shelled edamame

Coarse kosher salt and freshly ground black pepper

1 cup chunky salsa

1 tablespoon chopped fresh cilantro

1 jalapeño chile, cored, seeded, and chopped (optional)

1/2 cup light sour cream

1/2 cup plain 2 percent Greek yogurt

1 (4-ounce) can chopped chiles

1/2 cup grated reduced-fat Cheddar cheese (2 ounces)

4 green onions, trimmed and chopped

Calories 58
Fat 2 g
Carbs 6 g
Fiber 1 g
Protein 3 g

Place the beans in the bowl of a food processor fitted with the metal blade. Add the ground chiles and half of the lime juice. Pulse until smooth. Using a spatula, place the puree in the bottom of a 2-quart casserole dish to make the first layer. Set aside.

If the processor bowl is just a little bit dirty, and as long as you scraped out most of the beans into the serving bowl, go ahead and add the avocado, broccoli, and the remaining lime juice to the bowl. Season with salt and pepper. Process the guacamole until smooth. Spoon the guacamole on top of the beans to create the second layer.

In a small bowl, stir together the salsa, cilantro, and jalapeño. Pour the salsa mixture over the guacamole for the third layer.

In a small bowl, combine the sour cream and yogurt. Spoon the sour cream mixture on top of the salsa for the fourth layer. Pour over the chopped chiles for the fifth layer. Top with grated cheese and chopped green onions for the sixth and seventh layers. Serve immediately.

SMOKY EGGPLANT DIP

MAKES 2¹/₂ CUPS TO SERVE 10

Also known as baba ghanoush, this Middle Eastern dip is made from smoky, charred eggplant pureed with nutty, earthy tahini and copious amounts of extra-virgin olive oil. It's rich, silky, and absolutely one of my favorite summer dishes. The trouble is that the tahini (which is made of ground sesame seeds) and oil really move this vegetable dip into troublesome terrain. It seems so light, healthy, and full of great ingredients—but between the oil and ground seeds, it's really high in fat. Fat is fat. Some fat is better for you than others, but it's all about 120 calories a tablespoon.

Here, I've backed way off on the olive oil, but maintained the traditional earthy flavor and creaminess. Eggplant thrives in the Southern summer heat, and while this dish isn't typically Southern, it's a marvelous addition to the lightened up Southern table. Eggplant is available year round in grocery stores, but they taste their meaty, hearty best in the summer. Bonus is that in the warmer months, for a super intense smoky taste, you can pop them on the grill instead of cooking them in the oven.

2 pounds Italian eggplant

¹/₂ cup plain 2 percent Greek yogurt

1 tablespoon extra-virgin olive oil

1 tablespoon tahini or peanut butter (reduced-fat or all-natural)

4 garlic cloves, coarsely chopped

1 tablespoon lemon juice, plus more to taste

Coarse kosher salt and freshly ground black pepper

Fresh mint leaves, for garnish

Pomegranate seeds, for garnish

Whole-wheat pita triangles, for accompaniment

Vegetable crudités, for accompaniment

Preheat the oven to 450°F. Prick eggplants with a fork to pierce the skin and allow steam to escape while cooking. Place the eggplants in an ovenproof baking dish or cast-iron skillet. Cook in the oven until the skin of the eggplant is shriveled and the flesh has collapsed, about 30 minutes. Then, set the heat to broil and cook until charred on both sides, an additional 10 to 15 minutes.

Peel the eggplant and place the flesh in the bowl of a food processor fitted with the metal blade. Add just a piece or two of the charred skin, about the size of a couple of stamps. Add the yogurt, oil, tahini, garlic, and lemon juice. Season with salt and pepper. Puree until smooth, then taste and add more lemon juice or salt, if needed.

Transfer to a plate and garnish with mint and pomegranate seeds; serve with the pita triangles and crudités.

Calories 42
Fat 2 g
Carbs 5 g
Fiber 3 g
Protein 1 g

HOT MESS SPINACH *and* FETA DIP

MAKES 2 CUPS TO SERVE 16

This recipe was a struggle to lighten up, if I am going to tell you the absolute truth. You know what cheesy, greasy spinach dip tastes like. You've had it at countless parties. It's good, but not good for you. And, guess what? Pureed white beans, which are commonly used as a healthy "substitute" in spinach dip, taste nothing like the fantastically fatty combination of mayonnaise, cream cheese, and sour cream. Swapping in beans might work in some recipes, but not here. I'm happy to say I prevailed by using traditional ingredients but scaling back as much as possible on the mayo and sour cream. My secret for dealing with mayonnaise is to use half light mayonnaise and half plain 2 percent Greek yogurt. (I find the nonfat yogurt to be oddly chalky.) I've also amped up the nutrition by adding a carrot and used full-flavored Parmigiano-Reggiano and feta cheese. This dip is just cheesy enough, not greasy at all, and absolutely scrumptious.

1 (10-ounce) package chopped frozen spinach, thawed and well drained

1 carrot, peeled and grated on the fine side of a box grater

2 garlic cloves, very finely chopped

$1/3$ cup light sour cream

$1/3$ cup plain 2 percent Greek yogurt

$1/4$ cup light mayonnaise

$1/3$ cup lightly toasted pine nuts

Grated zest of 1 lemon

1 tablespoon lemon juice

$1/2$ cup freshly grated Parmigiano-Reggiano cheese (2 ounces)

Hot sauce

Coarse kosher salt and freshly ground black pepper

$1/2$ cup crumbled feta cheese (2 ounces)

Calories 70
Fat 5 g
Carbs 3 g
Fiber 1 g
Protein 4 g

Place an oven rack in the center position. Preheat the oven to 450°F. Spray a medium ovenproof baking dish with nonstick cooking spray. Set aside.

In a mixing bowl, combine the spinach, carrot, garlic, sour cream, yogurt, mayonnaise, pine nuts, lemon zest and juice, and $1/4$ cup of the Parmesan cheese. Add hot sauce to taste and season with salt and pepper. Spoon the mixture into the prepared baking dish and spread to an even thickness. Sprinkle the top with the remaining $1/4$ cup of Parmesan and the crumbled feta. Transfer to the oven and bake until the top browns and the dip heats through, 20 to 25 minutes.

Serve immediately.

TOASTING NUTS

A chef once told me there are three stages to toasting nuts: almost done, almost done, and burnt—but it doesn't have to be that way! I prefer to toast nuts in a dry skillet instead of toasting them in the oven, so they're under my watchful eyes. To toast nuts, simply place them in a single layer in a dry skillet. Heat the skillet over medium heat and cook, stirring occasionally, until fragrant and light golden brown, about 3 to 5 minutes. Once toasted, immediately remove them from the hot skillet to stop the cooking.

SLICE-*and*-BAKE
PARMESAN-HERB CHEESE STRAWS

MAKES 50 TO SERVE 25

My grandfather, whom I called Dede, used to make cheese straws for the holidays with his ancient, dinged-up, hand-cranked cookie press. I've taken his basic recipe and made a few adjustments to decrease the saturated fat, including substituting freshly grated Parmesan cheese to replace the extra-sharp Cheddar. Parmesan is not only richer and fuller in flavor than Cheddar; it's also dryer and best for baking in this satisfying salty snack.

I suggest using a silicone baking mat here—parchment paper works, but not as well. The dough is actually rolled out very thin, then cut into strips on the baking mat so they are extra-thin and crispy.

2 cups unbleached all-purpose flour

$1/2$ teaspoon fine sea salt, plus more for garnish

Pinch of cayenne pepper, plus more for garnish

1 teaspoon chopped fresh thyme

1 cup freshly grated Parmigiano-Reggiano cheese (4 ounces), at room temperature

$1/4$ cup ($1/2$ stick) unsalted butter, at room temperature

$1/4$ cup canola oil

$1/2$ cup 2 percent milk

Freshly ground black pepper, for garnish

Calories 93
Fat 5 g
Carbs 8 g
Fiber .3 g
Protein 3 g

Position the oven racks in the top and bottom thirds of the oven. Preheat the oven to 375°F. Set aside a rimmed baking sheet. Place a silicone mat on the work surface.

To make the dough, in a small bowl, combine the flour, salt, cayenne, and thyme. Set aside. In a heavy-duty mixer fitted with the paddle attachment, cream the cheese, butter, and canola oil on medium speed until smooth and well combined. Gradually add the flour mixture. Add the milk and mix on low speed until smooth. Cover the bowl with plastic wrap and set aside to rest for about 15 minutes. To shape the dough, work it in your hands; it should be soft and pliable (like Play-Doh).

Divide the dough into 3 pieces, about 7 ounces each. Working with 1 ball of dough at a time, place a ball of dough on the silicone mat. Using a rolling pin, roll out the dough to an $8^{1}/_{2}$ by 11-inch rectangle that is $1/8$ inch thick. Using a pizza cutter or a butter knife, cut the dough (without pressing so hard that you actually cut into the silicone mat) into long $1/4$-inch-wide strips. Transfer the entire mat with the strips on it to the reserved baking sheet. Season generously with salt, pepper, and additional cayenne pepper.

Bake the cheese straws, rotating the baking sheet once, until lightly browned on the edges, about 15 minutes. Remove the baking sheet to a rack to cool slightly. Using an offset or slotted spatula, separate the cheese straws and transfer to a rack to cool completely. Repeat with the remaining dough. Serve warm or at room temperature. Store up to 2 weeks in an airtight container.

GRILLED SHRIMP *and* PEPPER POPPERS

MAKES 8 TO SERVE 4

Most pepper poppers are pumped up with cheese, coated with bread crumbs, and deep-fried. I was inspired to nix the cheese and the deep fryer completely by my friends Julie and Charles Mayfield, health and fitness experts and the authors of *Quick & Easy Paleo Comfort Foods*. These pepper poppers are bright and coated with spices rather than soggy, heavy bread crumbs. I like to use fairly mild banana peppers and serve these as a first course. If you'd like to raise the heat, you can use jalapeño chiles, too. This recipe will fill about eighteen large jalapeño halves.

1 pound large shrimp (21/25 count), peeled, deveined, and chopped into $1/4$-inch pieces

$1/4$ teaspoon ground cumin

$1/2$ teaspoon ground coriander

$1/8$ teaspoon smoked paprika

2 tablespoons chopped fresh cilantro

Grated zest of 1 lime

Coarse kosher salt and freshly ground black pepper

4 Hungarian wax or banana peppers, halved lengthwise and cored

Calories 106
Fat 1 g
Carbs 4 g
Fiber 3 g
Protein 21 g

In a large bowl, combine the shrimp, cumin, coriander, smoked paprika, cilantro, and lime zest. Season with salt and pepper. Using a spoon, fill the peppers, mounding the shrimp over the top. (These may be made and refrigerated up to 1 day ahead.)

Prepare a charcoal fire using about 6 pounds of charcoal and burn until the coals are completely covered with a thin coating of light gray ash, 20 to 30 minutes. Spread the coals evenly over the grill bottom, position the grill rack above the coals, and heat until medium-hot (when you can hold your hand 5 inches above the grill surface for no longer than 3 or 4 seconds). Or, for a gas grill, turn all burners to high, close the lid, and heat until very hot, 10 to 15 minutes.

Place the peppers on the medium hot grill and cover. Cook until the peppers are tender, charred on the bottom, and the shrimp is cooked through and pink, 5 to 7 minutes.

Serve immediately.

LIGHTENED-UP PIMIENTO CHEESE

MAKES ABOUT 2 CUPS TO SERVE 16

My mother would sometimes make homemade pimiento cheese salad with the bright orange Cheddar coated in red wax, which my grandfather called "rat cheese," because it was often used to bait mousetraps. Only in the South would grated cheese and mayonnaise be considered a salad! As a small child, I considered pimiento cheese a decidedly grown-up flavor and didn't care for it in the least; it must have been those piquant jarred pimientos found at most Southern grocery stores. At some point, around middle school, it all changed. I'm not certain if it was a change in my palate or I wanted to emulate my mother, but I grew to love pimiento cheese.

It is traditionally served cradled in the curve of a celery stick. You can also employ bite-size cucumber cups, cored cherry tomatoes, or even slices of radish.

4 ounces extra-sharp Cheddar cheese, freshly grated (about 1 cup)

4 ounces light Cheddar cheese, freshly grated (about 1 cup)

1/4 sweet onion, grated

1 tablespoon light mayonnaise

1 tablespoon plain 2 percent Greek yogurt

2 tablespoons chopped pimientos, drained

Hot sauce

Coarse kosher salt and freshly ground black pepper

Japanese or English cucumbers, for accompaniment

Calories 52
Fat 4 g
Carbs .7 g
Fiber .1 g
Protein 4 g

To make the pimiento cheese, combine the cheeses, onion, mayonnaise, and yogurt in a bowl. Stir until well combined. Add the pimientos and hot sauce to taste. Season with salt and pepper and set aside.

Cut the cucumbers into 1-inch-thick rounds, discarding the ends, but leaving the skin on. Using a small spoon or melon baller, scoop the seeds and some of the flesh out of each round (be careful not to go all the way through) to form a small cup.

To serve, fill each cup with about 1 teaspoon of the pimiento cheese. Serve immediately.

CORNMEAL-CRUSTED CHICKEN BITES
WITH JALAPEÑO DIPPING SAUCE

MAKES 48 TO SERVE 8

Naturally gluten-free, these crispy, crunchy bites are a staple at our house during parties. You can substitute unbleached all-purpose flour if gluten isn't an issue or if you can't find chickpea flour. I really hope you'll take the extra step to toast and grind your own cumin seeds. Ground cumin out of a jar will never have the amazing, irresistible aroma of freshly ground spice, which is why I think whipping out the spice grinder is well worth the effort. Toasting the seeds releases the essential oils, and, when freshly ground, the flavor is aromatic and irresistible. But, hey, we all choose our battles, and it's still fragrant and rich with spices, even out of a jar. For an extra spicy kick, thinly slice the whole jalapeños, seeds and all.

This recipe makes a gracious plenty of dipping sauce, but you won't mind having extra around. Use it as a spread for sandwiches and wraps, a dip for vegetable crudités, or with chips and pretzels.

1 cup plain 2 percent Greek yogurt

1 tablespoon whole cumin seeds

²/₃ cup stone-ground yellow cornmeal, fine grind

²/₃ cup chickpea flour or unbleached all-purpose flour

1 teaspoon cayenne pepper

Coarse kosher salt and freshly ground black pepper

Organic nonstick cooking spray

6 boneless skinless chicken breasts or thighs cut into 1½-inch chunks (3 pounds)

3 cups loosely packed fresh cilantro leaves

4 green onions, trimmed and sliced

2 jalapeño chiles, cored, seeded, and chopped

Cornmeal-Crusted Chicken Bites
Calories 297
Fat 11 g
Carbs 14 g
Fiber 2 g
Protein 33 g

Line a fine-mesh sieve with cheesecloth and place over a bowl. Add the yogurt to the sieve and let drain until stiff, at least 1 hour.

Preheat the oven to 375°F. Line 2 rimmed baking sheets with silicone mats or parchment paper.

Toast the cumin seeds in a small dry skillet over medium heat until fragrant, 2 to 3 minutes. Remove from the heat and let cool. Pour into a spice grinder or a mortar and pestle and grind until a fine powder.

In a medium bowl or sealable plastic bag, combine the ground cumin seed with the cornmeal, chickpea flour, and cayenne pepper. Season with salt and pepper. Stir or shake to combine. Working in batches, add the chicken and stir or shake to combine and coat. Shake off the excess coating and place, without crowding, on the prepared baking sheets. Spray the chicken bites with nonstick cooking spray.

Place the pans in the upper and lower thirds of the oven. Bake 15 minutes, then flip the bites and rotate the baking sheets from top to bottom. Bake the chicken until the chicken is crisp and evenly brown, an additional 10 minutes.

Meanwhile, to make the sauce, in the bowl of a food processor fitted with the metal blade, combine the cilantro, green onions, and jalapeños. Puree until smooth. Transfer the drained yogurt to a small bowl

Jalapeño Dipping Sauce
per tablespoon
Calories 1
Fat 0 g
Carbs .2 g
Fiber .1 g
Protein .1 g

and whisk until silky smooth. Stir in the pureed cilantro mixture. Taste and adjust for seasoning with salt and pepper. You'll end up with 1½ cups of sauce.

Transfer the sauce to a serving bowl and place at the center of a platter, surrounded by warm chicken bites. Serve with toothpicks or skewers.

BARBECUE MEATBALLS

MAKES 32 TO SERVE 8

Everyone loves a meatball, including myself. Even vegetarians will make "meatballs" out of lentils! They are always a popular hors d'oeuvre at a party and can also easily be made ahead and reheated. For the family, Mama made a meatball with ground beef and Rice-a-Roni that we called "porcupines" (the rice in the mixture gave them a spiky appearance). And, I have a confession, I sometimes ask her to make them when I visit home. In this version, I sub the super grain quinoa in place of the rice and pasta, and leaner ground turkey for the traditional beef. I've also included a recipe for homemade barbecue sauce, but you can also use your favorite store-bought sauce.

2 tablespoons finely chopped sweet onion

1 pound ground turkey

$^1/_2$ cup cooked quinoa

2 tablespoons chopped fresh flat-leaf parsley

1 clove garlic, very finely chopped

Coarse kosher salt and freshly ground black pepper

1$^1/_2$ cups Sweet and Tangy Barbecue Sauce (recipe follows), heated

Barbecue Meatballs
Calories 155
Fat 8 g
Carbs 12 g
Fiber .5 g
Protein 11 g

Preheat the oven to 400°F. Set an ovenproof rack on a rimmed baking sheet. Spray with nonstick cooking spray and set aside. Place the onions in a ramekin or microwave-safe bowl and microwave on medium power until soft and translucent, about 25 seconds. Set aside to cool slightly. Meanwhile, in a large bowl, combine the turkey, onion, quinoa, parsley, and garlic. Season with salt and pepper. Stir to combine with a rubber spatula. (To taste and adjust for seasoning, simply cook a teaspoon or so of the mixture in the microwave.)

To form the meatballs, using a 1-ounce ice cream scoop or a tablespoon measure, scoop out the meat mixture and roll into a ball about the size of a walnut. Place onto the prepared rack. Repeat until all the meat mixture is used up. Transfer to the oven and cook until firm and the temperature reads 165°F on an instant-read thermometer, about 15 minutes. Remove from the oven and let cool slightly. (These can be made ahead up to this point and stored in an airtight container in the refrigerator for up to 3 days.)

Using a spatula, transfer the meatballs to a medium ovenproof baking dish. Pour over the barbecue sauce and shake the pan a bit to roll and coat the meatballs in the sauce.

Serve immediately or return to the oven and cook until the sauce is bubbly, about 10 minutes. Serve with toothpicks or skewers.

SWEET AND TANGY BARBECUE SAUCE

MAKES ABOUT 3 CUPS

1 teaspoon canola oil

$1/2$ sweet onion, very finely chopped

$1^1/_4$ cups reduced-sodium ketchup

1 cup apple cider vinegar

$1/4$ cup Worcestershire sauce

2 tablespoons Dijon mustard

1 tablespoon firmly packed brown sugar

Juice of $1/2$ lemon

1 tablespoon freshly ground black pepper, or to taste

Barbecue Sauce
per tablespoon
Calories 25
Fat .2 g
Carbs 6 g
Fiber .1 g
Protein .2 g

Heat the oil in a medium saucepan over medium heat. Add the onion and simmer until soft and melted, 5 to 7 minutes. Add the remaining ingredients. Bring to a boil, decrease the heat to simmer, and cook until flavors have smoothed and mellowed, about 10 minutes.

Store in an airtight container in the refrigerator. It will last for months.

CRAB *and* CELERY RÉMOULADE WRAPS

MAKES ABOUT 2 CUPS TO MAKE 16 WRAPS

Rémoulade is a fairly mild classic French mayonnaise-based sauce much like tartar sauce, but in Louisiana where I grew up, they kick it up a notch with paprika and a dose of cayenne pepper. I've lightened up the base and included a bit of horseradish for flavor, but not too much so it won't overpower the crab. This sauce is addictive and would be equally scrumptious with grilled shrimp or fish. Just remember, a dab will do ya!

Since childhood, I have loved crabbing. While vacationing on the coast, we'd cast nets baited with chicken necks off the dock and wait for the hungry crabs to swim in. Blue crabs are the classic Southern choice for this dish, but any sustainable lump crab meat will do.

2 tablespoons plain 2 percent Greek yogurt

2 tablespoons light mayonnaise

2 tablespoons Dijon mustard

2 stalks celery, sliced sharply on the diagonal into $1/8$-inch thick pieces

1 tablespoon freshly grated or prepared horseradish

1 tablespoon chopped fresh flat-leaf parsley

1 small shallot, finely chopped

1 garlic clove, finely chopped

Grated zest and juice of 1 lemon

1 teaspoon hot sauce, or to taste

$1/2$ teaspoon paprika

$1/4$ teaspoon cayenne pepper

1 pound lump crab, picked over for shells and cartilage

Coarse kosher salt and freshly ground black pepper

2 to 3 heads butter leaf lettuce, for accompaniment

Calories 19
Fat .6 g
Carbs 2 g
Fiber .4 g
Protein 1 g

In a large bowl, stir together the yogurt, mayonnaise, mustard, celery, horseradish, parsley, shallot, garlic, lemon zest and juice, hot sauce, paprika, and cayenne pepper. Add the crab and fold together as gently as possible. Taste and adjust for seasoning with salt and pepper.

To serve, spoon a tablespoon or so of the rémoulade into the lettuce cups and serve immediately.

DIRTY DOZEN

The Environmental Working Group (an organization of scientists, researchers, and policy makers) created a list called the "Dirty Dozen," which includes twelve foods that are particularly vulnerable to absorbing pesticides because of their soft skin. Celery, bell peppers, spinach, kale, collard greens, potatoes, and lettuce are all on the list, as are fruits like peaches, strawberries, apples, blueberries, nectarines, cherries, and grapes. The USDA tells us that consuming pesticides in small amounts won't harm you, but the EWG compiled lists using data from the USDA on the amount of pesticide residue found in nonorganic fruits and vegetables after they had been washed. The fruits and vegetables on the Dirty Dozen tested positive for at least forty-seven different chemicals. According to the a report issued by the American Academy of Pediatrics, "Children have unique susceptibilities to potential toxicity." Health experts suggest that when it comes to the Dirty Dozen list, choose organic, if it's available.

BAKED ONION BLOSSOM

MAKES 2 TO SERVE 6

One of my favorite spring dishes is Vidalia onions cooked in the microwave. Some recipes call for beef bouillon, too, but Mama always just cooked them with butter. Deep-fried onions are nearly two thousand calories each! Even sharing one onion among six people is a significant snack. This recipe is a mash-up of the two with just enough crispy and just enough soft, tender onion to satisfy. Make sure to use a sweet onion, preferably Vidalia, but others such as Texas Sweet, Walla Walla, and Maui will do as well.

2 sweet onions

Coarse kosher salt and freshly ground black pepper

2 tablespoons unsalted butter

2 tablespoons plain or whole wheat panko (Japanese) bread crumbs

1 tablespoon freshly grated Parmigiano-Reggiano cheese

1/2 teaspoon smoked paprika

1/2 teaspoon garlic powder

Calories 80
Fat 4 g
Carbs 10 g
Fiber 1 g
Protein 2 g

Prepare a large bowl of ice water.

Peel and remove the skin from the onions and trim the root and stem ends. Using a chef's knife, cut through the onion from the top down to the bottom, leaving the bottom intact, forming 16 wedges. Place the cut onions in the ice water, root side up. Set aside to soak for 30 minutes.

Preheat the oven to 425°F. Line a baking sheet with aluminum foil (for easy cleanup) and place a rack over the foil-lined baking sheet. Set aside.

Remove the onions from the water, pat dry with paper towels, and place on the prepared baking sheet, root side down. Using your fingers spread the onion "petals" to open and widen the "blossom." Season the onion with salt and pepper. Cover each onion with a sheet of aluminum foil, tucking it around the onion so it's a fairly tight fit. Transfer to the oven and bake until just tender, about 20 minutes.

Meanwhile, melt the butter. Set aside. In a small bowl, combine the bread crumbs, Parmesan, smoked paprika, and garlic powder. Season with salt and pepper. Remove the onion from the oven and remove the aluminum foil. With a pastry brush, coat the onions with the butter, then sprinkle with bread crumb mixture, using your fingers to get in the cracks and crevices of the onion.

Return the onion to the oven and bake, uncovered, until crispy tender, about 15 to 20 minutes.

Serve immediately.

CHAPTER 2

SALADS

and

SLAWS

BRIGHT, VIBRANT GREENS WITH SNAP; crunchy, colorful vegetables; freshly snipped herbs; savory, flavor-packed crumbles of cheese; and crunchy nuts tossed with a potent pop of pungent vinegar and a sensual ribbon of oil—now *that's* a salad! Mayo-less canned tuna on a dull, dry bed of greens—not so much. Fried chicken on a bed of greens drowning in ranch dressing—it could be tasty, but it is certainly not a good-for-you salad.

Salads don't have to be rabbit food, nor should they be drenched in unwholesome dressings or topped with secretly fatty "add-ons" that will derail your healthy eating. We think since we're on a diet we have to eat salad. First of all, one of my least favorite words is *diet*. It has such terrible connotations. It's a dismal part of our lexicon that signals what I can't have, not what I can have. Diets mean hunger and sad salads for days on end. That's no way to live!

This chapter is proof that you can fill your salad bowl with delicious food you actually want to eat. Make sure to start with a big bowl of greens as a base and mix it up. There are so many different varieties of lettuce and greens at the grocery store. My go-to-green is arugula because I love the spicy bite, but I'll occasionally interject some endive or romaine, depending on what looks good at the market. Take some time to slice, dice, and present the other vegetables you add to the mix. For example, chopped cucumbers have a different flavor and texture than shaved ribbons or snappy matchsticks. Play around a bit and come up with something interesting. Don't worry about your knife skills; salads don't have to be hard.

Make it easier for yourself by prepping in advance. After I score fresh, in-season vegetables at my local farmers' market, I wash, dry, chop, and store my haul in sealable reusable containers in the fridge. If I walk in the door hungry and can whip a salad together on the fly, it's a lot better for me than reaching for something less healthy. And store-bought, pre-cut carrot matchsticks, broccoli slaw, and undressed coleslaw are all great things to have at the ready in your vegetable bin.

As I suggested in my ten tips (see page 12), protein helps satiate hunger, so make sure to add lean protein to your salad. If you're looking for a non-meat protein alternative, add some peas, beans, chickpeas, edamame, quinoa, nuts, or leafy greens such as broccoli, spinach, and romaine lettuce. Another helpful tip is to go big or go home. Remember that hunger is the enemy. Pack it in! Vegetables and greens are great filler and can help curb your appetite.

This selection of salads includes a soulfully satisfying Bacon-Wilted Greens with Warm Pecan-Crusted Goat Cheese. Yes, you read that correctly: bacon and cheese. I'm a firm believer that you should use fattier, more calorie-dense ingredients judiciously, not omit them altogether. The key to a healthy lifestyle is moderation and portion control, not denying yourself all the things you love! This is why you'll see a crumble of bacon here or there, or a sprinkling of cheese. A little goes a long way, flavor-wise.

Need a ladies luncheon salad for a wedding or bridal shower? Try the Curried Shrimp Salad with Avocado and Orange or Asparagus and Baby Vidalia Onion Salad with Lemon-Tarragon Vinaigrette. How about a side salad to serve with sandwiches and wraps for the book club? I'll guarantee you'll be a best seller with the Apple-Raisin-Carrot Slaw. Don't forget that taking lunch to work is good for your wallet and good for your waistline. Great salads for brown bagging it include the Field Pea and Bean Salad with Tomato-Basil Vinaigrette, Shortcut Chicken Pasta Salad, and the Quinoa Cobb Salad with Green Goddess Dressing. Rabbit food? Pshaw. Let's hop to it!

A BIT OF BACON

Bacon—in a healthy cookbook? Yes, it's true. Lard, or pork fat, actually contains 40 percent of saturated fat (the "bad" fat) in comparison to 60 percent for butter. And lard's level of monounsaturated fat (a good fat) is 45 percent—nearly double that of butter—and about the same amount of polyunsaturated fat (another "good" fat) as olive oil! When you do eat bacon, make sure to go "whole hog" and get the good stuff that has a nice balance of meat, salt, and smoke. I like to cut my bacon into lardons, or matchstick-size pieces, before cooking. I find it's easier for cooking than crumbling. It also allows for the fat to render more completely from the meat so that I can pour off much of the grease and still maintain the smoky bacon flavor.

SHORTCUT CHICKEN PASTA SALAD

MAKES ABOUT 13 CUPS TO SERVE 8

Here's a new take on pasta salad that combines slow-roasted chicken, whole wheat pasta, and ready-to-go vegetables, such as shelled edamame, carrot matchsticks, and baby spinach. The light dressing is made with the juices of the chicken instead of additional oil and flavored with a hint of Dijon mustard. Baking the chicken on the bone increases the calories just a bit, but as a cook, I know that meat cooked on the bone is always more flavorful and tender. I bump up the nutritional content by adding finely chopped spinach.

Take a shortcut on a busy night by using a store-bought bird instead of roasting the chicken yourself.

4 (8-ounce) skinless bone-in chicken breast halves, or 4 cups skinless chicken pulled from a rotisserie chicken (about 16 ounces)

Coarse kosher salt and freshly ground black pepper

Juice of half a lemon

1 tablespoon pure olive oil

2 cups whole wheat penne pasta

2 cups broccoli florets

2 tablespoons light mayonnaise

2 tablespoons plain 2 percent Greek yogurt

1 tablespoon Dijon mustard

1 cup shelled edamame, thawed if frozen

1 cup matchstick carrots

1 cup baby spinach, very finely chopped

Calories 244
Fat 6 g
Carbs 19 g
Fiber 4 g
Protein 27 g

Preheat the oven to 350°F. Line a rimmed baking sheet with a silicone mat.

Season the chicken with salt and pepper and transfer the pieces to the prepared baking sheet. Drizzle on the lemon juice and oil, then bake the chicken until the juices run clear when pierced with a knife and the temperature measures 165°F when measured with an instant-read thermometer, about 40 minutes. Transfer the meat to a plate to cool, reserving the cooking juices.

Cook the pasta according to the package instructions, adding the broccoli to the pot for the last 2 minutes. Drain, reserving $1/4$ cup of the cooking water (plus 2 tablespoons more if you're using a rotisserie chicken that has no cooking juices).

Transfer the pasta and broccoli to a large bowl. Add the reserved cooking juices and pasta water and toss to coat the ingredients. When the chicken has cooled, pull the meat from the bone, tear it into bite-size pieces, and add it to the pasta.

In a small bowl, stir together the mayonnaise, yogurt, and mustard until well blended. Add the mixture, along with the edamame, carrots, and spinach, to the bowl and toss well. Taste and adjust the seasoning with salt and pepper. Serve immediately.

BACON-WILTED GREENS
WITH WARM PECAN-CRUSTED GOAT CHEESE

MAKES 5¹/₂ CUPS TO SERVE 6

Chèvre chaud, which translates to "hot goat cheese," is a traditional French dish that consists of a disk of fresh goat cheese melted on a bread crouton and served with crisp sturdy greens, often frisée. I first came across the idea of using a slice of apple instead of bread at a little *ferme d'auberge*, an inn that doubles as a working farm, in Burgundy, France. I can't imagine a French *bonne femme*, or housewife, being out of baguette, so maybe she simply had a bit of lightened up inspiration, too.

The traditional French version has a pretty slim greens-to-cheese ratio and is also dressed in a shallot vinaigrette, so I've lightened it up by adding tons of kale, using slightly less cheese, and eliminating the baguette. The result is still a hearty, filling salad packed with flavor and protein and perfect for fall.

2 center-cut bacon slices, cut into lardons (see note, page 36)

¹/₂ red onion, thinly sliced

1 apple, such as Gala, Granny Smith, or Honeycrisp, skin on, cored and diced

Coarse kosher salt and freshly ground black pepper

8 cups tender kale, stemmed and cut into chiffonade (see note, page 65)

1 tablespoon sherry vinegar

3 tablespoons very finely chopped pecans

1 (6-ounce) log goat cheese

1 small apple, such as Gala, Granny Smith, or Honeycrisp, skin on with core, cut crosswise into ¹/₄-inch-thick slices

Calories 255
Fat 16 g
Carbs 18 g
Fiber 4 g
Protein 14 g

Line a plate with paper towels. Line a rimmed baking sheet with a silicone mat and set aside.

Heat a large nonstick skillet over medium-high heat. Add the bacon and cook until crisp, about 5 minutes. Remove with a slotted spoon to the prepared plate. Pour off all but a film of the grease on the bottom of the pan. (Just eyeball it instead of trying to measure, but it should be just about ¹/₂ teaspoon; discard the remaining grease.)

To make the salad, return the skillet to low heat. Add the onion and the diced apple. Season with salt and pepper. Add the kale; cook until the kale begins to wilt, stirring occasionally, about 2 minutes. Add the vinegar; cover, and cook until just tender, stirring occasionally, about 4 minutes. Remove from the heat, taste, and adjust for seasoning with salt and pepper.

Meanwhile, preheat the oven to broil. Place the finely chopped pecans in a shallow dish and season with salt and pepper. Roll the goat cheese log in the pecans to evenly coat. Refrigerate until firm if necessary, then cut evenly into 6 rounds and place each round of cheese on the sliced apple. Place on the prepared baking sheet. Transfer to the oven and broil until the cheese is melted and browned, 3 to 5 minutes.

To serve, divide the kale salad among the plates. Top with an apple-cheese round and garnish with the reserved bacon. Serve immediately.

CURRIED SHRIMP SALAD
WITH AVOCADO AND ORANGE

SERVES 6

Curry makes me think of Indian cooking, but as a born and bred Southerner, it also brings to mind Junior League cookbooks and ladies who lunch. When I was a child, curry was still pretty exotic stuff and considered very "gourmet." Of course, when the ladies were dressing up dishes for company they would pull out the dusty bottle of curry powder.

On that note, my grandmother kept and mother still keeps all their spices in the freezer in order to retard their spoilage. However, sometimes those spices stayed around a little too long. Here's a helpful hint: The only spice McCormick's sells in the red and white tin is ground black pepper. If you have a tin of McCormick's spices that is *anything other* than black pepper, that tin was packaged before 1985.

Many seafood counters offer steamed shrimp and if you've had success with that, it's certainly a time-saver. However, sometimes they can be overcooked, which makes the shrimp dry, rubbery, and tough. The method in this recipe will ensure tender, flavorful shrimp, and the cooling technique I use to chill the cooked shrimp enhances its flavor instead of rinsing it away.

1 tablespoon finely chopped sweet onion

¹/₄ cup light mayonnaise

2 tablespoons finely chopped celery

1¹/₂ teaspoons curry powder (preferably Madras)

1 pound Boiled and Chilled Shrimp (recipe follows)

1 tablespoon chopped fresh flat-leaf parsley

1 tablespoon chopped fresh mint

Grated zest of 2 oranges (either navel or blood orange), with fruit set aside

Coarse kosher salt and freshly ground black pepper

1 avocado, seeded, and chopped (see note, page 41)

1 (5-ounce) container arugula

Finely grated zest and juice of 1 lemon

Coarse kosher salt and freshly ground black pepper

Place the onion in a medium microwave-safe bowl. Microwave on high just until the onion is tender, about 25 seconds. (Alternatively, you could sweat the onions in a small skillet with a mist of nonstick cooking spray, but one way or the other you want to cook the onions.) Let it cool slightly, then add the mayonnaise, celery, and curry powder. Stir to combine. Add the shrimp, parsley, mint, and grated orange zest. Season with salt and pepper. Set aside.

Have a small bowl at hand. To section the oranges, using a sharp knife and a cutting board, slice off the tops and bottoms of the oranges so they will stand upright. For each orange, set the fruit upright on the board. Working from top to bottom, slice off the peel, white pith, and outer membranes from the orange to expose the segments. Carefully cut each segment away from its membranes and put in the bowl along with any juice. Squeeze any remaining juice from the membranes into the bowl, and then discard them.

To assemble, combine the avocado, orange segments, and arugula in a medium bowl. Season with salt and pepper and toss to combine and coat. Pile the salad among 6 plates and top with a heaping spoonful of the curried shrimp. Serve immediately.

BOILED AND CHILLED SHRIMP

MAKES 1 POUND

12 cups water

1 carrot, coarsely chopped

1 stalk celery, coarsely chopped

1 lemon, halved

$^1/_2$ sweet onion

2 bay leaves, preferably fresh

1 tablespoon coarse kosher salt

1 pound unshelled medium shrimp (26/30 count)

Calories 224
Fat 13 g
Carbs 10 g
Fiber 4 g
Protein 20 g

Have ready a frozen freezer pack sealed in a heavy-duty plastic bag or a large heavy-duty zip-top plastic bag filled with ice cubes.

To poach the shrimp, combine the water, carrot, celery, lemon, onion, bay leaves, and salt in a large pot. Bring to a boil over high heat, then decrease the heat to low. Simmer gently for about 10 minutes to make a flavorful court-bouillon.

Meanwhile, make an ice bath to cool the shrimp: transfer several cups (or more, depending on the quantity of shrimp) of the broth to a large heatproof bowl. Place the ice pack in the bowl of broth; move the pack around until the broth is well chilled (drain and add more ice to the bag if needed).

Return the heat to high and bring the court-bouillon to a rolling boil. Add the shrimp and boil until the shells are pink and the meat is white, about 1 minute. Do not overcook. Drain the shrimp in a colander or remove with a slotted spoon, then immediately transfer to the chilled liquid in the ice bath to stop the cooking process. Peel and devein the shrimp.

HOW TO CUT AN AVOCADO

Grip the avocado with one hand. Using a chef's knife in the other hand, cut the avocado lengthwise completely around the seed. Twist to open the two halves to expose the pit. For safety, fold up a kitchen towel and use that to hold the avocado half with the pit. Gently tap the pit with a knife with enough force so that the blade of the knife wedges into the pit. Then, twist the pit out of the avocado and discard. (Mama often gets a seedling started by suspending the seed over water with toothpicks.) Using a small paring knife, make cuts in the avocado flesh in a crosshatch pattern, careful not to break through the avocado peel. Then, use a spoon to easily scoop out the avocado pieces.

ASPARAGUS *and* BABY VIDALIA ONION SALAD
WITH LEMON-TARRAGON VINAIGRETTE

SERVES 4

This salad absolutely sings spring. Asparagus has not traditionally been a Deep South crop, certainly not on a large scale. It requires a cold winter so that the plants can go dormant. The first time I saw asparagus growing was while visiting Thomas Jefferson's Monticello outside of Charlottesville, Virginia. I was shocked to see it comes straight up out of the earth, one spear at a time, just like someone stuck them in like darts in a dartboard.

Vidalia onions on the other hand, are a very common sight in the South—and one of my absolute favorite ingredients. Increasingly, in the spring you can find baby Vidalia onions, harvested before they reach maturity and essentially overgrown green onions. If you cannot find baby Vidalias, you may substitute green onions.

1¹/₂ pounds medium asparagus, trimmed

4 baby Vidalia onions, white and green parts, thinly sliced on the diagonal

Juice of ¹/₂ lemon

1 tablespoon sherry wine vinegar

2 tablespoons extra-virgin olive oil

1 English cucumber, partially peeled in strips, seeded, and cubed

3 tablespoons chopped fresh herbs (such as flat-leaf parsley, tarragon, chives, and mint)

Coarse kosher salt and freshly ground white pepper

Calories 139
Fat 7 g
Carbs 16 g
Fiber 6 g
Protein 5 g

Prepare an ice-water bath by filling a large bowl with ice and water. Line a plate with paper towels.

Bring a large pot of salted water to a boil over high heat. Add the asparagus and cook until bright green and just tender, about 3 minutes. Without draining, add the onions and cook until both vegetables are tender, an additional 30 or 45 seconds.

Meanwhile, in a small bowl, whisk together the lemon juice, vinegar, and oil. Set aside. Drain the asparagus and onions well in a colander, then set the colander with the asparagus and onions in the ice-water bath (to set the color and stop the cooking), making sure the asparagus is submerged. Once chilled, remove the asparagus and onions to the prepared plate. Pat dry and transfer to a large bowl. Add the cucumbers and herbs. Add the reserved dressing and toss to coat and combine. Taste and adjust for seasoning with salt and pepper. Serve immediately.

PUCKER UP!

Pack a lemon in your lunchbox. Use it to dress a salad, squeeze some into a glass of water instead of soda, enjoy it with some herbal tea, or even punch up leftovers with a pop of acid instead of salt.

FIELD PEA *and* BEAN SALAD
WITH TOMATO-BASIL VINAIGRETTE

MAKES 6 CUPS TO SERVE 6

This vibrant salad is best at the peak of summer when the vegetables are the best. When a Southerner hears the word "peas," they think of field or black-eyed peas, not English peas. Field peas come in a huge array of pod and seed color, size, shape, and flavor. Common types of field peas are crowders, creams, black-eyes, pink-eyes, purple hulls, and silver skins.

Here I've paired peas and butter beans with snap beans for a summer salad absolutely bursting with flavor. Use fresh in-season or frozen and thawed peas and beans for best flavor. Canned beans are often too mushy and nearly always astronomically high in sodium. Dry beans are more appropriate for fall and winter cooking, not this vibrant summer salad.

1 cup freshly shelled black-eyed peas (about ³/₄ pound unshelled) or frozen black-eyed peas, thawed

1 cup freshly shelled butter beans (about 1¹/₃ pounds unshelled) or frozen butter beans, not thawed

1 pound green beans, stem ends trimmed and snapped into 1-inch lengths

1 tomato, cored and chopped

¹/₂ sweet onion, very finely chopped

1 stalk celery, very finely chopped

1 garlic clove, very finely chopped

1 small bunch basil, stemmed and leaves very thinly sliced into chiffonade (see note, page 65)

2 tablespoons apple cider vinegar

1 teaspoon Dijon mustard

1 tablespoon best-quality extra-virgin olive oil

Coarse kosher salt and freshly ground black pepper

Calories 155
Fat 3 g
Carbs 28 g
Fiber 8 g
Protein 6 g

Bring a large pot of salted water to a rolling boil over high heat. Add the black-eyed peas and butter beans. Decrease heat to simmer and cook just until tender, about 25 minutes. (Taste one and see how tender it is; the cooking time will depend on their freshness.) In the same pot, add the green beans and continue to cool until crisp-tender, about 3 minutes.

Meanwhile, prepare an ice-water bath by filling a large bowl with ice and water. Drain the peas and beans well in a colander, then set the colander with beans in the ice-water bath (to set the color and stop the cooking), making sure the beans are submerged. Drain the beans, shaking off the excess water, and transfer to a large bowl. Add the tomato, onion, celery, garlic, and basil.

To make the dressing, whisk together the vinegar and mustard in a small bowl. Add the oil in a slow steady stream, whisking constantly, until the dressing is creamy and emulsified. Season the dressing with salt and pepper.

To serve, drizzle the dressing over the bean mixture, then toss to coat. Taste and adjust for seasoning with salt and pepper. Serve immediately.

GRILLED POTATO SALAD
WITH BACON VINAIGRETTE

MAKES 3 CUPS TO SERVE 6

Oh, my, this potato salad is decadent and delicious. I know what you're thinking—"again with the bacon?!" It's true, bacon is high in fat, but used in moderation, it can amazingly improve the flavor of a dish. And it adds about 125 calories to this entire salad, only about 20 calories per serving. So, the lesson is if you *do* eat bacon, I say treat it like a seasoning ingredient, not to shingle a sandwich.

The two-step process of cooking the potatoes might seem a bit tedious, but it transforms this summer salad from same-old to sublime. If all the other ingredients are ready to go, it's quite simple to toss them on the grill with whatever else you might be grilling.

1¹/₂ pounds baby Yukon gold potatoes, (about the size of a walnut), halved

Coarse kosher salt and freshly ground black pepper

3 slices center-cut bacon, cut into lardons (see note, page 36)

1 garlic clove, mashed into a paste with salt (see note, page 113)

2 tablespoons apple cider vinegar

1 teaspoon firmly packed brown sugar

3 tablespoons pure olive oil

4 whole green onions

2 tablespoons chopped fresh flat-leaf parsley, plus more for garnish

Calories 175
Fat 9 g
Carbs 23 g
Fiber 3 g
Protein 4 g

Line a plate with paper towels and set aside.

Place the potatoes in a medium saucepan and cover by about 2 inches with cold water. Add salt and bring to a boil over medium-high heat. Boil gently until the potatoes are tender enough to pierce easily with a knife, about 15 minutes. Don't overcook them or they will fall apart. (I prefer using boiling water, but you can also microwave them until tender. Place the potatoes in a microwave-safe covered dish and season with salt and pepper. Cover and cook on high until just tender, about 8 minutes depending on the strength of your microwave. Carefully drain off any water the potatoes exuded during cooking. Return the cover to the pot and let the potatoes steam, 5 to 7 minutes. Proceed with recipe.)

Drain the potatoes in a large colander and let cool. Meanwhile, cook the bacon in a large skillet over medium heat, stirring occasionally, until crisp, about 5 to 7 minutes. Drain on the prepared plate.

Remove all but about 2 teaspoons of the bacon drippings from the pan. Off the heat, add the garlic, vinegar, and brown sugar to the drippings in the pan, scraping up any browned bits. Whisk in 2 tablespoons of the oil and season with salt and pepper. Set aside.

Prepare a charcoal fire using about 6 pounds of charcoal and burn until the coals are completely covered with a thin coating of light gray ash, 20 to 30 minutes. Spread the coals evenly over the grill bottom, position the grill rack above the coals, and heat until

CONTINUED

medium-hot (when you can hold your hand 5 inches above the grill surface for no longer than 3 or 4 seconds). Or, for a gas grill, turn all burners to high, close the lid, and heat until very hot, 10 to 15 minutes.

Transfer the potatoes to a bowl. Add the remaining tablespoon of oil and toss to coat. Working in batches, grill the potatoes cut-side down on the grill until they have developed a light char, 2 to 3 minutes. Grill the onions until they are charred, 4 to 6 minutes a side. Chop the green onions into 1-inch pieces and add to the bowl with the potatoes. (If there are any larger pieces of onions, cut them into smaller pieces). Add the reserved bacon vinaigrette and parsley. Toss to coat. Let all sit for a few minutes to allow the flavor to penetrate the potatoes. Sprinkle with reserved bacon and toss to coat. Taste and adjust for seasoning with salt and pepper. Serve immediately.

DIG IT

Potatoes have a bad reputation in low-carb and paleo diets, but that doesn't mean they're bad for you. They're a good source of fiber, especially if you eat the skin. There are three basic categories of potatoes: starchy, all-purpose, and waxy. Starchy potatoes are great for baking. Because of their starch, they don't hold together very well when boiled. They have a light, mealy texture and are fluffy and absorbent, perfect for a baked potato. Examples of starchy potatoes include russet and Idaho. All-purpose potatoes include Yukon golds and purple Peruvians. They do a good job holding their shape, but share many traits in common with high-starch potatoes. Yukon golds make excellent mashed potatoes. Waxy potatoes are best for salads, as they hold their shape while boiling. They also work well in dishes like soups or stews when you want cubed potatoes. Examples of these types of potatoes include red bliss, Irish, and fingerling.

BROCCOLI SLAW
WITH LIGHT BUTTERMILK RANCH

MAKES 4 CUPS TO SERVE 6

A bag of broccoli slaw can be a weeknight lifesaver. The bag lasts a bit longer than fresh salad greens, makes a great slaw with no chopping or dicing required, and it's packed with good-and-good-for-you broccoli stems and crispy carrots. Keep a bag of undressed broccoli slaw in the refrigerator to add texture and bulk to salads, for stir-fries, or even to use as a crunchy sandwich topper.

Broccoli slaws are a stand-by at family reunions and "dinner on the grounds," the church supper potluck where the ladies divide and conquer to feed the masses. Traditionally, it is topped with deep-fried ramen noodles—which are high in calories, fat, and carbohydrates—so I skip the noodles and instead top with healthier, but still deliciously crunchy, almonds.

Speaking of processed foods created to survive doomsday (I'm looking at you, packaged ramen noodles), I love ranch dressing, but I really don't love ingredients I cannot pronounce. Make this light, fresh ranch dressing from scratch and you'll kick the bottle for good.

3 tablespoons light mayonnaise

3 tablespoons plain 2 percent Greek yogurt

2 tablespoons low-fat buttermilk

1 green onion, trimmed and chopped

1 tablespoon chopped fresh flat-leaf parsley

1 tablespoon rice vinegar

1 teaspoon Dijon mustard

1 garlic clove, very finely chopped

Coarse kosher salt and freshly ground black pepper

1 (10-ounce) bag broccoli slaw

1 cup sliced napa cabbage

6 radishes, thinly sliced

¼ cup roasted unsalted almonds, chopped

In a bowl, combine the mayonnaise, yogurt, buttermilk, green onion, parsley, vinegar, mustard, and garlic; season with salt and pepper. Add the broccoli slaw, cabbage, radishes, and almonds; toss to combine and coat. Taste and adjust for seasoning with salt and pepper. Cover with plastic wrap and chill for up to 8 hours until ready to serve. Taste and adjust for seasoning once again before serving.

Calories 142
Fat 5 g
Carbs 20 g
Fiber 7 g
Protein 6 g

SASSY SLAW

MAKES 4 CUPS TO SERVE 6

One of the most heinous crimes of my childhood was to sass my mama. Still is. Believe me, "talking back" and "being sassy" did not go over well, at all. My sweet little mama is a whole lot of power in a tiny package. One raise of one eyebrow was enough to put the fear of the Lord in my sister and me. I was raised saying "yes, ma'am" and "no, sir." I'm still pretty old-fashioned that way, although I now simultaneously giggle and grimace when those terms of respect are used with me.

While a sassy child is a definitely no-no, this sassy slaw packs just the right amount of panache, with its hearty splash of apple cider vinegar and a double dose of mustard. I suggest making the dressing first, then setting it aside so you can chop your vegetables.

$^1/_4$ cup apple cider vinegar

2 tablespoons sugar

1 teaspoon Dijon mustard

$^1/_4$ teaspoon mustard powder

$^1/_4$ teaspoon celery seed

2 tablespoons canola oil

$^1/_4$ large green cabbage (about 1 pound), cored and finely shredded (about 3 cups)

$^1/_4$ large red cabbage (about 1 pound), cored and finely shredded (about 3 cups)

1 large carrot, grated

1 green onion, trimmed and chopped

$^1/_2$ jalapeño chile, cored, seeded, and chopped

2 tablespoons chopped fresh flat-leaf parsley

Coarse kosher salt and freshly ground black pepper

Calories 95
Fat 5 g
Carbs 13 g
Fiber 2 g
Protein 1 g

In a small saucepan, combine the vinegar, sugar, mustard, mustard powder, and celery seed. Heat over medium heat until the sugar has dissolved. Set aside to cool slightly. Add the oil and whisk to combine.

In a large bowl, combine the green and red cabbage, carrot, green onion, jalapeño, and parsley and toss to combine. Pour over the reserved slightly cooled dressing. Taste and adjust for seasoning with salt and pepper. Refrigerate until chilled, about 15 minutes. Toss, taste and adjust for seasoning again, then serve immediately.

QUINOA COBB SALAD
WITH GREEN GODDESS DRESSING

SERVES 6

I'm sure you've all ordered cobb salad at a restaurant, and been served a huge plate with each individual ingredient laid out in a long mound, concealing the greens underneath. I love this fancy *salade composée* presentation, especially with my fancy French training, but unfortunately, huge mounds of chicken, egg, bacon, and cheese aren't great for people who are trying to watch what they eat. To achieve the same flavor, but to back off a bit on the calories and fat, I suggest tossing it together like a chopped salad. Four ounces of chicken per person doesn't look like much, especially if you are used to eating a whole boneless chicken breast, which is closer to eight ounces. However, when it is chopped and blended, you taste the chicken without registering that it's a smaller portion. I've also snuck in a bit of quinoa. Quinoa is a complete protein containing all eight essential amino acids. It's light and fluffy in texture, but has that whole grain power to fill up. This salad is substantial and great for a light summer supper.

There's nothing quite like freshly prepared homemade salad dressing, especially one as fresh and flavorful as Green Goddess. You can substitute store-bought rotisserie chicken for the breasts if you'd like, just make sure to remove and discard the skin.

4 sprigs thyme

2 bay leaves, preferably fresh

1 teaspoon whole black peppercorns

3 boneless skinless chicken breasts (about 1 1/2 pounds)

Coarse kosher salt and freshly ground black pepper

1/2 cup quinoa, rinsed

2 slices center-cut bacon, cut into lardons (see note, page 36)

2 hard-cooked eggs

1 heart of romaine, chopped

12 grape tomatoes, halved

Green Goddess Dressing (recipe follows)

Line a plate with paper towels. Set aside.

To cook the chicken, bring a large pot of salted water to a rolling boil over high heat. Add the thyme, bay leaves, and peppercorns. Decrease the heat to simmer.

Season the chicken breasts on both sides with salt. Add to the gently simmering liquid, and cook until firm and the juices run clear when pierced with a knife, 10 to 12 minutes. Set aside to cool and rest, reserving 1 cup of the poaching water. Using a chef's knife, dice the cooked chicken into cubes about 1/2 inch thick. Set aside.

Rinse the quinoa in a fine sieve until water runs clear, drain, and transfer to a medium pot. Add the reserved 1 cup of poaching water and 1 teaspoon of salt; bring to a boil. Cover, decrease the heat to medium-low and simmer until the water is absorbed, 15 to 20 minutes. Set aside off the heat for 5 minutes; uncover and fluff with a fork.

CONTINUED

QUINOA COBB SALAD WITH GREEN
GODDESS DRESSING, CONTINUED

Calories 272
Fat 9 g
Carbs 17 g
Fiber 4 g
Protein 31 g

Meanwhile, to cook the bacon, heat a large skillet over medium heat. Add the bacon and cook until crisp and brown, 5 to 7 minutes. Using a slotted spoon, transfer the bacon to the paper towel-lined plate. Set aside.

Halve the eggs and discard one of the yolks. Chop the remaining 2 whites and 1 yolk into $1/4$-inch pieces. Set aside.

To assemble the salad, in a large bowl, combine the romaine, quinoa, reserved bacon, reserved eggs, tomatoes, and reserved chicken; season with salt and pepper. Serve with dressing on the side.

GREEN GODDESS DRESSING

MAKES $3/4$ CUP

$1/4$ cup light mayonnaise

$1/4$ cup plain 2 percent Greek yogurt

1 anchovy fillet

1 teaspoon Dijon mustard

1 green onion, trimmed, and chopped into 1-inch pieces (white and pale green only)

2 garlic cloves

1 sprig fresh mint, leaves only

2 sprigs tarragon, leaves only

10 fresh chives, cut into 1-inch pieces

$1/2$ cup loosely packed flat-leaf parsley leaves

Coarse kosher salt and freshly ground black pepper

1 tablespoons apple cider vinegar

In the jar of a blender or in the bowl of a food processor fitted with the metal blade, combine the mayonnaise, yogurt, anchovy fillet, mustard, green onion, garlic, mint, tarragon, chives, and parsley. Season with salt and pepper. Process a bit, then to get the mixture really going, add the vinegar. Process until smooth, scraping down the sides of the jar or bowl with a rubber spatula, as necessary. Taste and adjust for seasoning with salt and pepper. Store in an airtight container in the refrigerator for up to 3 days.

Green Goddess Dressing
Calories 20
Fat 1 g
Carbs 1 g
Fiber .2 g
Protein .7 g

APPLE-RAISIN-CARROT SLAW

MAKES 8 CUPS TO SERVE 8

North Georgia is famous for its apple orchards, and one of our favorite fall pastimes is to drive up into the mountains and buy apples for the winter. We find all the familiar varieties, like Red and Golden Delicious, in addition to some not always available in many chain grocery stores, like Rome, Gala, Winesap, and Mutsu. Hard winter apples have lower water content than summer apples and will last longer. It's important to take them out of the bag due to the ethylene gas, which hastens ripening. Loose apples will last in the refrigerator or in a cool cellar for 6 to 8 weeks.

This slaw is a mash-up of apple-raisin and carrot-raisin slaw. Conventional poppy seed dressing is creamy and rich because it typically is a whopping cup of oil emulsified into $1/2$ cup of vinegar and nearly that amount of refined sugar. Yikes! Here I have kept things velvety smooth with the triple threat of light sour cream, yogurt, and light mayonnaise.

$1/4$ cup light sour cream

$1/4$ cup plain 2 percent Greek yogurt

3 tablespoons light mayonnaise

$1^1/2$ tablespoons white balsamic vinegar

1 tablespoon poppy seeds

1 teaspoon mustard powder

1 Rome apple, skin on, cored, and chopped (about 2 cups)

$3/4$ cup golden raisins

1 (16-ounce) package cabbage-and-carrot coleslaw (or $1/2$ small green cabbage, cored and finely chopped, and 2 carrots, grated)

Coarse kosher salt and freshly ground black pepper

Calories 124
Fat 3 g
Carbs 23 g
Fiber 3 g
Protein 3 g

In a small bowl, stir together the sour cream, yogurt, mayonnaise, vinegar, poppy seeds, and mustard powder to combine. In a medium bowl, combine the apple, raisins, and coleslaw. Pour the dressing over the vegetable mixture and stir to combine. Taste and adjust for seasoning with salt and pepper. Serve immediately or store in an airtight container in the refrigerator for up to 2 days.

CHAPTER 3

FROM
the
GARDEN

SOME OF MY MOST treasured photos are of me toddling behind my grandparents in their garden. As an adult, I still love vegetable gardening. Ours seems to get larger every year. There's something indescribably satisfying about planting seeds, then harvesting and cooking from a plot of land you've tended.

This is not a case of me having a green thumb. I am not very good with houseplants. I can barely keep the hearty houseplant pothos alive, which could likely survive nuclear winter and Sahara-like drought, but vegetables? Oh, I love to dig in the dirt. The taste of a tomato fresh off the vine is like no other. The tenderness of freshly picked summer squash and the fiery, floral heat of a chile seared by the summer sun are worth every shovel of dirt.

But you don't have to grow your own vegetables to be interested in what you eat and how it's produced. Studies show that more and more consumers are seeking out foods that are better for their families as well as the environment. Organic farming promotes healthy soil, biodiversity, and

the conservation of water. It helps keep chemicals out of the air, earth, and water. Organic farmers focus on utilizing renewable resources. Makes a whole lot of sense to me that if you are taking care of your body, you will want to take care of the earth, too.

Organic produce is grown without synthetic fertilizers, herbicides, and pesticides. The USDA strictly enforces organic production and handling. (Organic meat and dairy livestock receive no antibiotics, added hormones, and are raised on organic feed.) No organic products are ever irradiated or tagged with the letters "GMO" (genetically modified organism). GMO fruits and vegetables are altered in a laboratory using molecular genetic engineering techniques such as gene cloning or protein engineering. This is in the news a lot and there are vehement opinions on both sides.

Whether you go "green" or conventional, you need to make sure you get two to three cups of vegetables a day, as recommended by the USDA on ChooseMyPlate.gov—or more if you're trying to lighten up. I find it's best to eat with the seasons.

The food is fresher and just tastes better. Summer produce is the embodiment of an easy, breezy sunny day. Ripe tomatoes are sliced. Okra only needs a short simmer or perhaps a bit of grilling. Fresh corn takes a quick dip in salted, boiling water and is eager and ready for a soft, melting—and judicious—dab of butter. Fall brings wet mornings and long cool nights. Fall produce can be more challenging, but has its own glorious colors, flavors, and textures. As the days grow shorter, dark greens replace the tender lettuces and easy vegetables of spring and summer. The dark leafy greens, gnarled root vegetables, and hard winter squash of fall are more complex than sunny summer produce and need more components to balance their flavors.

This chapter is bursting with vibrant vegetable recipes to enjoy throughout the year, and many are made with seven or so ingredients, making them easy on the wallet. And, if you need some time-saving shortcuts, you can "hack" your way with prechopped vegetables, including onions, carrots, celery, tomatoes, greens, and even butternut squash. Don't limit yourself to vegetables only for supper. Say "yes!" to vegetables for breakfast, lunch, and dinner. One of my favorite breakfast dishes is Collard Greens with Chipotle Potlikker topped with an over-easy farm egg. Give Oven-Fried Okra a try for a party snack and Roast Sweet Potato and Pears with Blue Cheese for a filling and satisfying lunch. Want an enlightened Sunday supper? Try the "new Southern" vegetable plate of Creamed Corn–Stuffed Tomatoes, Green Beans with Candied Garlic, and Spicy Eggplant Stir-Fry, a mouth-watering combination without a squeal of pig in sight.

PAN-ROASTED ASPARAGUS *and* MUSHROOMS

SERVES 4

I have a confession. Until very recently, I never really liked fresh asparagus. Bigger confession. I actually like canned asparagus. My grandmother always had a couple of the familiar silver cans in her cupboard for "salad" or to be heated with a can of sliced mushrooms and a knob of butter for a side dish for company.

We've lost sight of the seasonality of asparagus and mushrooms because they are always in the grocery store, but both are spring crops—so make this recipe when they really are most plentiful. Asparagus and mushrooms also have a natural affinity. This dish works well with plain old white button mushrooms as well as cremini or oyster, and is exceptionally splendid if you want to gild the lily with chanterelles or porcini.

1 tablespoon pure olive oil

1 pound mushrooms, sliced

Coarse kosher salt and freshly ground black pepper

1 shallot, sliced

1 garlic clove, sliced

1 pound asparagus, ends trimmed and stalks cut into 1½-inch pieces

½ cup homemade chicken stock (see note, page 78) or reduced-fat, low-sodium chicken broth

Finely grated zest of 1 lemon

Calories 74
Fat 4 g
Carbs 8 g
Fiber 2 g
Protein 5 g

Heat the oil in a large skillet over medium-high heat. Add the mushrooms and season with salt and pepper; cook, stirring often, until tender and no longer squeaky, about 3 minutes. Add the shallot and garlic and cook until fragrant, 45 to 60 seconds. Add the asparagus and stir to combine. Add the chicken stock and cover with a tight-fitting lid. Cook until just tender, 3 to 5 minutes, depending on the thickness of the asparagus. Remove the lid and increase the heat to high to reduce the stock. Cook, stirring constantly, until the liquid has glazed the vegetables and the asparagus is tender, 1 to 2 minutes. Add the lemon zest and stir to combine. Taste and adjust for seasoning with salt and pepper. Serve immediately.

THE FIFTH TASTE

Taste experts refer to five basic flavors: sweet, salty, sour, bitter, and umami, often translated as "savory." Think of the meaty flavor of sautéed mushrooms, a juicy steak, or a rich stock. Umami is actually used in various forms all over the world. Umami is found in beans and grain, fermented products, mushrooms, and cured meats. When you can wield umami in your kitchen to enhance and bolster flavor, it allows you to lessen the emphasis on fat, sugar, and salt. Umami-rich foods satiate more readily, and enable you to eat less. In the wise words of my fellow Georgian, Julia Roberts, in *Steel Magnolias*, "I would rather have thirty minutes of wonderful than a lifetime of nothing special." Think of umami as what makes food wonderful, and use it to make flavors pop—and help you lighten things up.

SPRING PEA, LEEK, *and* CAULIFLOWER "COUSCOUS"

MAKES 7 CUPS TO SERVE 6

My dear friend and mentor Nathalie Dupree has an ancient, battered *couscoussière* from her far-flung travels. It's a curved, two-pot steamer; while the stew simmers in the lower pan, the steam rises into the upper pot to cook the couscous. When I first started working for her as a novice apprentice, it seemed as exotic as the moon!

Couscous is not a grain, but a fine pasta. It is deceptively light and it feels like it should be exceptionally healthy, but regular pasta is actually slightly more nutritious. This "couscous" isn't really couscous at all but grated cauliflower! It makes a light and lemony dish, a perfect accompaniment to grilled chicken or seafood.

1 head (32 ounces) cauliflower, outer leaves removed, halved, and cored

1 tablespoon pure olive oil

2 small tender leeks, cut into rings, well washed

1 stalk celery, diced

1 cup shelled English peas

$1/2$ cup dry white wine

$1/4$ cup water

Pinch freshly grated nutmeg

Finely grated zest of 1 lemon

1 tablespoon unsalted butter, at room temperature

$1/4$ cup freshly grated Parmigiano-Reggiano cheese (1 ounce)

2 tablespoons chopped fresh mint

Coarse kosher salt and freshly ground white pepper

Calories 134
Fat 6 g
Carbs 14 g
Fiber 5 g
Protein 6 g

Using the large-hole side of box grater, grate the cauliflower into rice-size pieces. The yield should be about 8 cups. Set aside.

Heat the oil in a large nonstick skillet over medium-low heat. Add the leeks and celery; cook until the white of the leeks is soft and translucent and the green is bright, about 5 minutes. Add the peas and grated cauliflower and cook for 2 minutes, stirring occasionally.

Add the white wine and water and cook, stirring occasionally, until the vegetables are tender and the liquid has evaporated, about 8 minutes. Remove from the heat and add the nutmeg, lemon zest, butter, cheese, and mint. Stir to combine. Taste and adjust for seasoning with salt and pepper. Serve immediately.

SAUTÉED GREEN BEANS *with* SUMMER CORN

SERVES 6

When my grandfather grew corn down by the river, it seemed to all come in at once. We would sit on the front porch in the still, stifling heat of the evening and shuck corn. Good Lord, it was hot! Everything seemed to move in slow motion, especially for a fidgety kid who had lost interest in helping after the fifth ear. Well, that was until a large black snake slithered out of the burlap sack that held the harvested corn and headed toward my grandmother. I'm not certain I had ever seen her move so fast. I think it was very shortly after that incident that she made my grandfather dump the corn out of the sack under the carport and bring it to her on the porch, one well-searched bucket at a time.

3 ears fresh sweet corn, shucked and silks removed

1 pound green beans, stemmed

1 teaspoon pure olive oil

1/2 sweet onion, very finely chopped

Coarse kosher salt and freshly ground black pepper

1 tablespoon chopped fresh basil

Calories 98
Fat 2 g
Carbs 20 g
Fiber 3 g
Protein 4 g

Prepare an ice-water bath by filling a large bowl with ice and water. Bring a large pot of salted water to a rolling boil over high heat. Add the corn and beans and cook until the beans are crisp-tender, about 3 minutes. Drain well in a colander, then set the colander with beans and corn in the ice-water bath (to set the color and stop the cooking), making sure the beans and corn are submerged.

Remove the corn from the ice bath and pat dry with a paper towel. Cut the corn kernels from the cob and set aside.

Heat the oil in a large skillet over medium-high heat. Add the onion and cook until soft and translucent, 3 to 5 minutes. Drain the green beans and add to the onions. Add the reserved corn and season with salt and pepper. Cook, stirring to combine, until heated through and the flavors have combined. Add the basil and stir to combine and coat. Taste and adjust for seasoning with salt and pepper. Serve immediately.

CREAMED CORN-STUFFED TOMATOES

SERVES 6

Creamed corn is one of summer's most precious gifts. I spend a lot of time in New England where I was told all about the sweet summer corn. "Our corn is the best in the world." In my mind, I silently dismissed it. "Oh, okay," I responded, the half acknowledgment that conveys the unspoken sentiment, "You really don't know what the hell you are talking about." Best in the world? Yankee corn? Seriously? Well, let me tell you. It *is* the best corn I have ever tasted.

You'll notice I'm calling for gluten-free bread crumbs here; they are available in gourmet grocery stores and larger stores like Whole Foods Market, but you can also use wheat bread crumbs, if you like. While I don't have any issues with wheat, a member of my family does, as well a handful of other dietary issues. I try very hard to be inclusive with my cooking and if she's eating with us, then I make those changes for all of the dishes. It's not that hard to make adjustments if you have the information, and it's far more hospitable for everyone to enjoy the same meal.

6 medium tomatoes

2 teaspoons pure olive oil

Scraped kernels from 4 ears fresh sweet corn (about 2 cups kernels)

1 poblano chile, cored, seeded, and finely chopped

Coarse kosher salt and freshly ground black pepper

3 tablespoons freshly grated Pecorino-Romano cheese

1 teaspoon chopped fresh thyme, plus optional sprigs for garnish

1/4 cup gluten-free bread crumbs

Calories 124
Fat 4 g
Carbs 20 g
Fiber 4 g
Protein 5 g

Preheat the oven to 350°F. To form tomato shells, with a serrated knife, slice off the tops of the tomatoes and remove their cores. Using a melon baller or a spoon, scoop out the seeds and pulp of the tomatoes to create a shell, transferring the juices and pulp to a small bowl. Using your hands, squish the pulp and seeds until smooth but slightly chunky. Set aside.

Meanwhile, to make the filling, heat the oil in a large skillet over medium heat. Add the corn and poblano and season with salt and pepper. Cook, stirring occasionally, until the corn is tender, 8 to 10 minutes. Add the reserved tomato mixture and cook until it's absorbed into the corn and the skillet is dry, stirring occasionally, about 3 minutes. Add the grated cheese and chopped thyme. Taste and adjust for seasoning with salt and pepper.

Arrange the tomato shells, cut-side up, in a small casserole dish. For each tomato shell, spoon in some filling (about 1/3 cup each, depending on the size of the tomato). Sprinkle over the gluten-free bread crumbs.

Bake the tomatoes until the filling is heated through, the tomato shells are tender, and the topping is golden brown, 20 to 25 minutes. Serve immediately.

SPICY EGGPLANT STIR-FRY

SERVES 6

Eggplant is one of summer's most luscious and sensuous vegetables and has always been one of my favorites both to eat and to grow. And, while eggplant readily belongs in both Italian and Far Eastern cuisine, it suits our hot Southern climate, as well. My grandparents always had the brilliant, jewel-like, nearly black-purple vegetable in their garden.

Eggplant is very meaty in texture, which adds bulk to a meal. Feeling hungry is a surefire way to stray from a healthy eating; I like to eat vegetables with substance, such as eggplant, so I don't feel deprived. The trouble is that eggplant will soak up oil like a sponge if given the chance. It's necessary to first salt the eggplant to help remove the moisture, making the flesh less sponge-like and denser. Plus, it needs quick cooking over high heat, as in this Asian-inspired stir-fry.

2 medium globe or 4 small Asian eggplants, skin on, cut into 1-inch pieces

2 tablespoons coarse kosher salt

2 teaspoons canola oil

1 sweet onion, chopped

1 red bell pepper, cored, seeded, and chopped

2 garlic cloves, finely chopped

1/2 teaspoon red pepper flakes

2 tablespoons reduced-sodium soy sauce

3 leaves fresh basil, sliced in chiffonade (see note, below)

Freshly ground black pepper

Calories 87
Fat 2 g
Carbs 15 g
Fiber 4 g
Protein 3 g

Sprinkle the eggplant generously with salt and let them sit in a colander for about 30 minutes to drain. Rinse the eggplant under cold running water to remove the salt, then firmly squeeze a few pieces at a time in the palm of your hand to draw out almost all the moisture. Pat the eggplant dry with a clean kitchen towel and set aside on a plate.

Heat 1 teaspoon of the oil in a large nonstick skillet over medium heat. Add the onion and red bell pepper. Cook, stirring occasionally, until the onion is soft and translucent, 3 to 5 minutes. Add the garlic and red pepper flakes; cook until fragrant, 45 to 60 seconds. Transfer to a bowl and keep warm.

Add the remaining teaspoon of oil to the skillet and place over high heat. Add the eggplant and cook, tossing occasionally, until tender and golden, about 10 minutes. Return the sautéed-onion mixture and stir to combine. Add the soy sauce and basil and toss to coat and combine. Taste and adjust for seasoning with salt and pepper. Serve immediately.

CHIFFONADE

To *chiffonade* means to thinly slice an herb or leafy green into ribbons. To do this, stack the leaves on top of each other, tightly roll them into a cylinder, then slice crosswise into thin strips.

GREEN BEANS *with* NEW POTATOES
AND CANDIED GARLIC

SERVES 6

Old-school beans and potatoes are most often nearly cooked to pablum and served swimming in bacon grease. There's a time and place for that, but not when we are lightening things up! If it's more likely to help you get in the kitchen, go ahead and purchase the peeled cloves in the produce department. This caramelized garlic is good on these beans, on meats, and yes, even just on a spoon.

8 ounces small new potatoes, about the size of a walnut

1 pound green beans, stemmed

$1/2$ cup garlic cloves

2 tablespoons pure olive oil

1 tablespoon balsamic vinegar

1 cup water

1 tablespoon firmly packed dark brown sugar

Coarse kosher salt and freshly ground black pepper

Calories 117
Fat 5 g
Carbs 17 g
Fiber 3 g
Protein 3 g

Make an ice-water bath by filling a large bowl with ice and water. Line a plate with paper towels.

To cook the potatoes, place them in a large pot of salted water and bring to a boil over high heat. Cook until just tender to the point of a knife, about 15 minutes, depending on the size of the potatoes. Add the beans and cook until crisp-tender, about 3 minutes. Drain the potatoes and green beans well in a colander, then set the colander in the ice-water bath (to set the color and stop the cooking), making sure the beans and potatoes are submerged. Once chilled, remove the beans to the prepared plate.

Meanwhile, place the garlic cloves in a small saucepan and cover with water. Bring to a boil over medium-high heat. Decrease the heat to simmer. Cook for 3 minutes to remove the initial bitterness of the garlic, then drain well and pat dry.

Dry the saucepan with a kitchen towel—make sure you do this very well to prevent the oil from popping—and drizzle 1 tablespoon of the olive oil in the saucepan. Add the balsamic vinegar and the water (be careful, it will spit and spew at you as the water hits the hot oil), and bring to a boil. Add the garlic and simmer, stirring occasionally, for 10 minutes. Then add the sugar and simmer on medium heat until most of the liquid has evaporated and the garlic is caramelized, about 15 minutes.

Heat the pot used to cook the beans and potatoes over high heat. Add the reserved beans and potatoes. Cook, stirring constantly, to reheat the vegetables. When they are hot, pour the caramelized garlic and any of the cooking liquid over the bean-potato mixture. Stir to combine and coat. Taste and adjust for seasoning with salt and pepper. Serve immediately.

OVEN-FRIED OKRA

SERVES 6

I love okra. It is one of those vegetables that people either love or hate. The only symbol of okra armistice is crispy, crusty fried okra. Even rabid okra haters will admit to tolerating fried okra. (After all, people will get on board with deep-fried *anything*.) Let's face it, there's really nothing like fried okra, but this oven-fried version does a darn good job of coming close. And, technically, I suppose this okra dish should really be called oven-baked, but that's not nearly as seductive, now is it?

1 cup stone-ground yellow cornmeal

$^1/_4$ teaspoon cayenne pepper

Coarse kosher salt and freshly ground black pepper

$^1/_2$ cup low-fat buttermilk

1 large egg, lightly beaten

1 pound fresh okra pods, stemmed and cut into $^3/_4$-inch slices

Organic nonstick cooking spray

Calories 110
Fat 2 g
Carbs 21 g
Fiber 4 g
Protein 4 g

Place a rimmed baking sheet oven in the oven. Preheat the oven to 450°F. Combine the cornmeal and cayenne pepper in a shallow dish. Season heartily with salt and pepper; set aside.

Whisk together the buttermilk and egg in a large bowl. Add the okra and season with salt and pepper. Stir to combine and set aside to coat, about 3 minutes.

Using a slotted spoon, remove the okra from the buttermilk mixture and add to the cornmeal. Dredge okra in the cornmeal mixture. Remove the hot baking sheet from the oven and spray with cooking spray. Place the coated okra on the heated pan and lightly coat the okra with additional cooking spray. Bake for 25 minutes, stirring once. Stir and spray again. Cook until crispy and dark golden brown, 10 to 12 additional minutes. Remove from the oven and season with salt and pepper. Serve immediately.

SLIME BUSTERS

The folks who despise okra are put off by the slime, sometimes more politely called mucilage. Personally, I think mucilage sounds pretty scary, but no matter what you call it, here are five cooking tips to bust the slime.

- Choose small pods; wash and thoroughly dry them.
- If cutting into pieces, wipe your knife on a kitchen towel between slicing so as not to spread the slime.
- Give it some room! Don't crowd the pan when cooking, as the steam will produce more slime.
- Cook okra at high heat and cook it fast.
- Don't cover okra while cooking.

SUMMER SQUASH CASSEROLE

MAKES 8 CUPS TO SERVE 8

There are many variations of this Southern staple: church lady recipes that use cans of "cream of" soup, Junior League egg-mayo combinations, and chef-y versions with heavy cream and bread crumbs. I've lightened up this old-school Southern favorite and suggest preparing a béchamel sauce with low-fat milk, to which I add a combination of reduced-fat and regular Cheddar cheese. It is far less fatty and rich than the traditional version—and still tastes delicious. When preparing summer squash dishes, I like to mix the squash varieties for an interesting contrast of color.

4 zucchini squash, sliced $1/4$ inch thick (about 1 pound)

3 yellow squash, sliced $1/4$ inch thick (about 1 pound)

$1/2$ sweet onion, chopped

$1/2$ cup freshly grated 50 percent reduced-fat Cheddar cheese (2 ounces)

$1/2$ cup freshly grated sharp Cheddar cheese (2 ounces)

1 tablespoon canola oil

1 tablespoon unbleached all-purpose flour

$3/4$ cup 2 percent milk, warmed

Coarse kosher salt and freshly ground black pepper

2 large eggs, lightly beaten

1 cup fresh whole wheat bread crumbs (from about $1^{1}/2$ slices of bread)

$1/4$ cup chopped mixed fresh herbs (such as flat-leaf parsley, chives, and basil)

Calories 125
Fat 6 g
Carbs 11 g
Fiber 2 g
Protein 9 g

Preheat the oven to 350°F. Lightly coat a medium ovenproof casserole dish with nonstick cooking spray. Bring a pot of salted water to a rolling boil over high heat. Place the zucchini, yellow squash, and onion in a steamer basket and set over the boiling water; steam until the squash is just tender, about 5 minutes. (You can also place all of the squash in a microwave-safe bowl and zap it on high power until tender, about 4 minutes, depending on the strength of your microwave.) Drain away any excess water and pat the squash dry with a kitchen towel. Set aside.

Combine the grated cheeses. Measure out $3/4$ cup of the mixed cheeses for the sauce; set aside the remaining $1/4$ cup of cheese for the topping.

Heat the oil in a saucepan over medium heat. Add the flour and, stirring constantly, cook until very pale blonde, about 1 minute. Add the milk and whisk until smooth. Bring to a boil, whisking constantly, over high heat. Remove from the heat. Add the reserved $3/4$ cup of cheese to the sauce and stir to combine. Taste and adjust for seasoning with salt and pepper.

Pour over the squash and onion; stir to combine. Add the eggs, half of the bread crumbs, and the herbs. Transfer to the prepared casserole. Combine the remaining $1/2$ cup bread crumbs and the remaining $1/4$ cup of cheese. Sprinkle on top of the squash mixture. Bake until firm and brown on top, about 30 minutes.

Remove to a rack to cool slightly, then serve.

BE S.M.A.R.T

When you are making choices, it's important to set S.M.A.R.T goals, ones that are specific, manageable, attainable, realistic, and time-bound (set to a specific period of time). It's no good to say, "I wish I looked like I did in college." There's not much about you that's the same as it was when you were twenty, and a whole lot you are probably glad is not! One way or the other, wishing won't make it so. It is realistic to understand that safe, attainable weight loss happens at one to two pounds a week. So, if you want to lose twenty pounds, it's very likely going to take at least ten to twenty weeks—and that's staying on track, on target, on point. Knowing that going in will help you stick to the plan!

GRATE IDEAS

Shred a block of cheese rather than using the purchased preshredded cheese in a bag. Freshly shredded cheese has more moisture, so it melts more smoothly and retains a bolder, more pronounced flavor. Also, instead of using all reduced-fat cheeses, use a combination of reduced fat and regular. Reduced fat cheeses don't melt as easily and are sometimes lacking in flavor. Mixing it up allows for great meltability and trims some of the fat at the same time. I prefer the Cabot brand of cheese over many of the other reduced-fat brands; they offer both 75 percent and 50 percent reduced-fat Cheddar.

SUMMER SQUASH "LASAGNA"

SERVES 8

I posted a photo of this dish on Facebook while testing recipes for this book and it lit up my page like fireworks on the Fourth of July—everyone wanted the recipe. I had to make them wait, but here it is! There's absolutely nothing like gooey, cheesy goodness. It's also the siren call that can crash your best-laid plans to lose weight on the rocks. In this recipe, I use tender summer squash instead of lasagna noodles to lighten things up in a most flavorful way. The squash is paired with a simple marinara sauce layered with a judicious, yet still luxurious, amount of cheese for ultimate flavor. It's not saying "no" to pasta, it's saying "yes" to vegetables!

Keep that in mind in the summer when so many vegetables are in season and you have the grill fired up. Try grilling the vegetables for this lasagna for a bit of extra smoky flavor. And, while you are at it, grill extra vegetables to enjoy the entire week and store them in an airtight container. You can chop them up and put in a salad or a wrap.

8 medium zucchini or yellow squash (about 3 pounds), stemmed and cut lengthwise into $1/4$-inch-thick strips

Coarse kosher salt and freshly ground black pepper

1 cup part-skim ricotta cheese

$1/4$ cup plus 1 tablespoon freshly grated Parmigiano-Reggiano cheese (1.25 ounces)

2 garlic cloves, very finely chopped

$1/4$ teaspoon red pepper flakes

2 tablespoons chopped fresh herbs (such as basil, oregano, and flat-leaf parsley)

1 cup best-quality prepared marinara sauce

10 ounces part-skim mozzarella cheese, grated

Calories 197
Fat 10 g
Carbs 11 g
Fiber 2 g
Protein 16 g

Preheat the oven to 425°F. Line 2 rimmed baking sheets with silicone mats or parchment paper. Place the squash on the prepared baking sheets in a single layer. Season with salt and pepper. Roast, rotating the baking sheets once, until the squash is tender, about 25 minutes. (Leave the oven on after vegetables are cooked.) Remove the vegetables to a rack to cool slightly.

Meanwhile, spray an 8 by $11^1/2$-inch baking dish with nonstick cooking spray. In a bowl, combine the ricotta, $1/4$ cup of the Parmesan, garlic, red pepper flakes, and herbs. Season with salt and pepper and stir to combine.

Place $1/2$ cup of marinara sauce in the bottom of the prepared baking dish. Layer with half of the vegetables. Top with the ricotta mixture, spreading with a spoon to cover the vegetables completely. Top with $1/4$ cup of the marinara and spread to cover. Layer with the remaining vegetables and top with the remaining $1/4$ cup of marinara. Top with grated mozzarella and sprinkle over the remaining tablespoon of Parmesan. Transfer to the oven and cook until bubbly and golden brown, 25 to 30 minutes. Remove to a rack to cool slightly, then serve.

BAKED ZUCCHINI CRISPS

MAKES 60 PIECES TO SERVE 6

My grandmother used to stand at the stove and fry slices of squash and zucchini in her cast-iron skillet. She'd dip thick rounds of squash in egg then coat them in a combination of seasoned cornmeal and flour. They'd bubble furiously in the fat, transforming from pale yellow disks to golden brown coins. Using her well-worn two-pronged fork, she would transfer them, one at a time, to layers of split-open brown paper bags to drain. It seems they never made it to the table. My sister, cousins, and I would hover round the kitchen table like little birds with mouths wide open, our greasy little fingers scarfing down the crispy rounds as soon as they would cool enough to touch.

I've found that oven-baking squash yields the same delightful, crunchy texture—with a fraction of the fat. Serve with mustard or warm marinara for a crispy side dish.

2 large egg whites, lightly beaten

2 medium zucchini, stemmed and sliced $1/4$ inch thick

Pinch of cayenne pepper

Coarse kosher salt and freshly ground black pepper

2 cups panko (Japanese) bread crumbs

$1/2$ cup freshly grated Parmigiano-Reggiano cheese (2 ounces)

2 teaspoons fresh thyme leaves

Organic nonstick cooking spray

Calories 112
Fat .2 g
Carbs 22 g
Fiber 1 g
Protein 5 g

Preheat the oven to 425°F. Line two rimmed baking sheets with silicone mats. Place the egg whites in a large bowl and beat with a whisk until frothy. Add the zucchini slices and cayenne pepper. Season with salt and pepper and stir to combine and coat.

In a shallow dish, combine the panko, Parmesan, and thyme. Season with salt and pepper. Dip each squash round into the panko mixture, coating it evenly on both sides, pressing the coating to stick. Place them in a single layer without touching on the prepared baking sheets. Spray lightly with nonstick cooking spray. Transfer to the oven and bake until golden brown and crispy, rotating top to bottom, about 25 minutes. Using a metal spatula, immediately remove the crisps to a rack to cool slightly (and to prevent them from becoming soggy) before serving.

BRAISED COLLARDS
IN TOMATO-ONION GRAVY

SERVES 6

A few years ago, I was visiting my cousin Gene and his wife, Kathy, in Fort Valley, Georgia, and teaching a class at a local cooking school. We needed collard greens, so I told the owner I needed two bunches. She drove down the street to a pickup truck parked nearby and came back with two "bunches." Well, these bunches easily contained two or three monster-size bundles, so big that I had to hug them with both hands. We laughed for hours about the size of Fort Valley collards.

Traditional Southern collards are cooked with fatback, ham hock, or bacon grease. There's a lot of flavor in that fat, so when you eliminate it, you need to bump up the flavor elsewhere. Charring the tomatoes before adding them to the gravy is a great way to add a smoky, umami-rich note without adding fat or calories.

4 ripe, medium Roma tomatoes, cored

2 teaspoons canola oil

1 sweet onion, chopped

3 garlic cloves

Coarse kosher salt and freshly ground black pepper

16 cups chopped collard greens (1 pound)

Calories 72
Fat 2 g
Carbs 11 g
Fiber 5 g
Protein 4 g

Heat a medium skillet over high heat. Add the cored tomatoes and cook until they are charred on all sides, about 5 minutes. Remove to the bowl of a food processor fitted with the metal blade.

Let the skillet cool slightly by taking it off the heat or decreasing the heat, depending on how smoking-hot your skillet is. Have the heat at low and add the oil (the skillet will still hold a great deal of heat). Add the onion and garlic, and sauté, stirring occasionally, until both are a deep golden-brown, 8 to 10 minutes. Remove from the heat and let them cool slightly. Transfer to the food processor bowl containing the reserved charred tomato, and process until smooth. Transfer the mixture to a large saucepan. Cook over medium-low heat until thickened, 5 to 7 minutes. Season with salt and pepper.

Add the chopped collards and cook until just tender, 15 to 20 minutes. Taste and adjust for seasoning with salt and pepper. Serve warm.

COLLARD GREENS *with* CHIPOTLE POTLIKKER

SERVES 6

Instead of smoky bacon or fatback and hot sauce, how about we skip the meat and keep the heat? This recipe has become a family favorite for a weeknight side dish. Chipotles are smoked jalapeño chiles and can be found dried whole or canned swimming in a spicy adobo sauce that is made from a combination of chipotles, tomatoes, and other spices for a rich, often smoky, flavor. *Adobo* is Spanish for marinade. You can find canned chipotles in adobo in the international or Hispanic section of most major supermarkets.

Transfer any unused chiles and the sauce to a sealable glass container. (The brick-red sauce will stain plastic and permeate the container with the spicy aroma.) Refrigerate for up to 4 weeks or try freezing individual chiles with some of their sauce in an ice cube tray and then transfer the cubes to a sealable freezer container. Frozen, they'll keep for about 3 months.

2 cups homemade chicken stock (see note, below) or reduced-fat, low-sodium chicken broth

1 sweet onion, sliced

4 garlic cloves, halved

1 chipotle in adobo

1 tablespoon adobo sauce

Coarse kosher salt and freshly ground black pepper

12 cups chopped collard greens (about 12 ounces)

Calories 57
Fat 1 g
Carbs 10 g
Fiber 4 g
Protein 4 g

In a medium saucepan, bring the stock, onion, garlic, chipotle, and adobo sauce to a boil over high heat. Season with salt and pepper. Decrease the heat to simmer and cook until the onion is soft and translucent, about 5 minutes. Add the greens and cover. Cook, stirring occasionally, until the greens are tender, 15 to 20 minutes. Taste and adjust for seasoning with salt and pepper. Serve immediately.

HOMEMADE CHICKEN STOCK

Chicken stock couldn't be easier to make at home. If you save vegetable scraps (carrot and celery tops, for example) and chicken carcasses (from whole roasted chickens) in a bag in your freezer, you can combine them to make an easy stock. Or you can start fresh: combine 2 pounds of chicken wings or bones, 3 chopped celery stalks, 3 chopped carrots, 3 chopped onions, 2 bay leaves (I prefer fresh), 2 sprigs of flat-leaf parsley, 2 sprigs of thyme, 4 to 6 black peppercorns, and 14 cups of water in a large stock pot. Bring the mixture to a boil over high heat, then decrease to low and simmer for $1\frac{1}{2}$ hours, skimming the foam off the top as it rises. Strain through a colander, then store in an airtight container in the refrigerator for up to 1 week, or freeze for up to 3 months. Before using, skim off and discard any fat that has risen to the surface.

BRUSSELS SPROUTS *with* RAISINS AND PECANS

SERVES 6

Sour, salty, bitter, sweet, and savory all come together to make these brussels sprouts an astonishingly good side dish. When left whole, it's often best to parboil the sprouts. They can also be peeled layer by layer, for a quick-cooking stir-fry, but that can be quite time-consuming. The method used here of slicing these miniature cabbages is the best of both worlds—and is even quicker if you have a mandoline.

1 teaspoon pure olive oil

16 ounces brussels sprouts, trimmed and sliced $\frac{1}{8}$ inch thick

Coarse kosher salt and freshly ground black pepper

3 garlic cloves, halved

1 cup homemade chicken stock, (see note, page 78) or reduced-fat, low-sodium chicken broth

2 tablespoons golden raisins

1 tablespoon balsamic vinegar

2 tablespoons chopped pecans

Calories 77
Fat 3 g
Carbs 9 g
Fiber 3 g
Protein 3 g

Heat the oil in a large skillet over medium-high heat until shimmering. Add the sprouts and season with salt and pepper. Cook, stirring occasionally, until the sprouts are beginning to char and still bright green, about 3 minutes. Add the garlic and cook until fragrant, 45 to 60 seconds. Add the stock and raisins; cook, stirring occasionally, until the pan is nearly dry and the sprouts are just tender, 8 to 10 minutes. Add the balsamic vinegar and pecans. Stir to combine. Taste and adjust for seasoning with salt and pepper. Serve warm.

ROASTED SWEET POTATO *and* PEARS

SERVES 4

Our family home had an ancient, gnarled, and knotty pear tree on the property. I believe it was some form of an heirloom Bartlett, but the true name of the fruit was long lost. Every fall my grandfather would harvest the pears and my grandparents would preserve the golden, tapered orbs in sugar syrup or combine them with savory ingredients such as onion and spices for pear chow-chow, a traditional Southern fruit relish made with end-of-season fruits and vegetables. Pears are one of fall's sweetest gifts. The season is more fleeting than apples and they don't have as long of a shelf life. Pears must be enjoyed during that short time or preserved, as my grandparents did, for future enjoyment.

The honey-rich flavor of pear marries wonderfully with the earthy sweetness of the sweet potato in this side dish, bringing to mind the expression "what grows together, goes together." I'm finishing the combination of their mutual sweetness with a smattering of blue cheese crumbles for a hint of salt and spice.

2 large sweet potatoes, sliced, or 1 pound small sweet potatoes, cut into $1/4$-inch-thick slices

1 pear (such as Bosc), cored and into $1/4$-inch-thick slices

1 tablespoon unsalted butter, melted

3 sprigs fresh thyme, leaves only

Coarse kosher salt and freshly ground black pepper

$1/2$ teaspoon sherry vinegar

2 ounces blue cheese, crumbled

Preheat the oven to 350°F. Combine the potato and pear in a medium gratin dish or ovenproof skillet. Pour over the butter, scatter over the thyme leaves, and season with salt and pepper. Toss to combine. Transfer to the oven and bake until the potatoes are tender, about 45 minutes. Remove from the oven and drizzle over the vinegar and blue cheese crumbles. Stir to combine. Taste and adjust for seasoning with salt and pepper. Serve immediately.

Calories 199
Fat 7 g
Carbs 30 g
Fiber 5 g
Protein 5 g

PAN-SEARED WINTER SQUASH

SERVES 4

I'm most accustomed to roasting squash in the oven. Mama slow-roasts acorn squash halves filled with butter, maple syrup, and pecans to absolute candy sweetness. This recipe mirrors the flavors of that classic dish, but with far less butter and sugar. The bonus is that the natural sugar in the slices becomes mottled with a series of deep golden brown circles when pan-seared; it's gorgeous. It's then finished in the oven with a few whole sprigs of thyme and bay leaves scattered between the pieces to enhance the savory flavor. Lastly, just a drizzle of maple syrup and a smattering of pecans finish the dish. This will become your guaranteed go-to dish for fall.

1 tablespoon canola oil, plus more if needed

1 acorn squash (left unpeeled), seeded and cut into eighths

4 to 6 (unpeeled) butternut squash slices, cut 1/4 inch thick (6 ounces)

1 small red onion, stem end trimmed and root attached, cut lengthwise into eighths

Coarse kosher salt and freshly ground black pepper

2 bay leaves, preferably fresh

2 fresh thyme sprigs, leaves only

2 tablespoons maple syrup

2 tablespoons chopped pecans

Calories 147
Fat 6 g
Carbs 24 g
Fiber 3 g
Protein 2 g

Preheat the oven to 350°F. Brush a large skillet with oil and heat over medium heat. Add the squash pieces without crowding and cook on both sides until mottled and browned, 2 to 3 minutes per side. Transfer to a bowl. (You will need to sear the vegetables in 2 to 3 batches, depending on the size of your skillet.) Repeat with remaining oil and squash.

Return all of the squash to the skillet and season with salt and pepper. Drizzle over any remaining oil. Tuck the onions and herbs around the vegetables in the skillet and transfer to the oven. Bake until tender to the point of a knife, about 35 minutes. Remove from the oven and drizzle over the maple syrup and sprinkle over the pecans. Return to the oven to warm the syrup and lightly toast the pecans, additional 5 minutes. Remove the herbs and serve immediately.

CHAPTER 4

GRAINS, GRITS,

and

OTHER STARCHY GOODNESS

A GOOD RULE TO LIVE BY is that if you don't love it, don't eat it. Don't like that mushy, overwrought grain dish you picked at the hot buffet in an attempt to be healthier? Don't eat it. It's your body; treat it well. When most people hear the phrase "treat yourself," they think about pigging out on a pint of ice cream or taking a "splurge day." But a big part of treating yourself is treating yourself *right*—taking care of your body, and enjoying foods that will help you thrive. Treat yourself by taking the time to prepare delicious, wholesome food that you actually want to eat— don't just eat throwaway "diet" food because you think you're supposed to.

Rice and grits can be part of a healthy eating meal plan. Both are staples that have a long legacy in traditional Southern cuisine. Ground corn in the form of grits is simple country food. Most Southerners love grits and I am no exception. When I was a little girl, my family would travel from our home in Louisiana to Georgia for holidays to visit our family. My father would drive through the

night as my sister and I slept in the back of the big, green Oldsmobile with its expansive back seat. It was a production moving a family across four states; the car was packed to the gills and even had a bulging cargo box on the roof. My sister and I fought sleep—and each other—for as long as we could. As the sun rose, we would stop for breakfast at a truck stop on the Georgia-Alabama border.

I remember Mama rousing us from our deep sleep and kneeling over the backseat to dress her drowsy brood. My sister and I twisted and turned, trying to get the right arm in the right sleeve and our knotty heads brushed. Eventually, we were appropriately clothed and entered the doors next to the flashing neon sign. The bright florescent lights in the diner caused me to squint after the long, dark night. Tall, weathered men in baseball caps sipped coffee and smoked cigarettes at the counter. It was another universe. My sister and I squirmed in the shiny green vinyl booths trying to see as much as possible of this strange, foreign world. Soon enough, a lady with big hair would come along and say, "Here ya' go, honey" and place a steaming hot bowl of cheese grits on the worn Formica table in front of me. Suddenly, the alien landscape would disappear and I was home. Grits mean home to me.

Of course, those grits were swimming in cheese and melted butter—a delicious but unfortunately decadent detail that doesn't make sense for a healthy eating plan. But grits are important to me and many Southerners; I just had to find a way to lighten them up. My recipe for a Southern Style Shepherd's Pie with Grits uses whole-grain grits, chicken, and spinach for a healthy, savory layered casserole. I've also included a little side note for a basic recipe on how to cook grits.

Rice plays a huge part in the Southern diet, especially in Louisiana, where rice farms dot the bayou, and in the South Carolina Low Country. White rice is the most common choice; however, white rice has had the bran removed and is not as nutritious as whole-grain brown rice. For that reason, I've tried to focus mostly on whole grains for the recipes in this book. Whole grains are high in fiber and have been linked to a lower risk of heart disease, diabetes, certain cancers, and other health problems. It's exciting to see so many options on the grocery store shelves—and if you see a whole grain you're not familiar with, I encourage you to experiment.

RED BEANS *and* GREENS

SERVES 8 TO 10

I asked my friend Pableaux Johnson, New Orleans native and Creole food authority, about adding finely chopped collard greens to the classic Cajun dish red beans and rice to up the nutritionals. He replied, "Beans and greens sounds like a Virginia Willis original. It's like adding curry and fish to a gumbo and saying 'It's a Curry-Fish Gumbo!' Somewhere in there, the natural DNA of the dish has been changed." Serving it on top of quinoa might get me chased out of N'awlins! But it doesn't mean this dish is wrong. One bite and I'm sure you will agree.

1 tablespoon canola oil

12 ounces chicken or turkey andouille sausage, sliced

2 sweet onions, chopped

2 celery stalks, chopped

2 poblano chiles or green bell peppers, cored, seeded, and chopped

Coarse kosher salt and freshly ground black pepper

6 to 8 cloves garlic, very finely chopped

1 pound red beans, soaked overnight

10 cups water

$^1/_2$ teaspoon cayenne pepper

$^1/_4$ teaspoon white pepper

$^1/_4$ teaspoon smoked paprika

3 bay leaves, preferably fresh

1 cup coarsely chopped collard greens, finely chopped (about 4 ounces)

3 green onions, trimmed and chopped

Hot sauce

Coarse kosher salt and freshly ground black pepper

Cooked quinoa, for accompaniment

Heat the oil in a large heavy pot over medium-high heat. Add the sausage and cook until browned, about 5 minutes. Add the onion, celery, and chiles. Season with salt and pepper. Cook until the onions are soft and translucent, 3 to 5 minutes. Add the garlic and cook until fragrant, 45 to 60 seconds.

Drain the soaked red beans and add the beans to the pot. Cover with the fresh water. Add the cayenne, white pepper, smoked paprika, bay leaves, and collard greens. Bring the mixture to a boil, then decrease the heat to simmer. Cook, stirring occasionally, until the beans are tender, 1 to 1$^1/_2$ hours. When the beans are tender, using a potato masher, mash in the pot to break up some of the beans. Stir in the chopped green onions and season well with hot sauce to taste. Taste and adjust for seasoning with salt and pepper.

To serve, ladle into warmed bowls with cooked quinoa with additional hot sauce on the side.

Calories 256
Fat 6 g
Carbs 35 g
Fiber 9 g
Protein 16 g

NEW SOUL CREOLE DIRTY RICE

MAKES 4 CUPS TO SERVE 6

This old-school Louisiana rice dish is traditionally made with giblets, liver, and ground pork. It's simple country cooking, using up any spare bits and pieces of meat. It's also typically very rich and fatty. This recipe achieves those same meaty flavors, but is far healthier, lighter, and nutritionally dense with a cup of collard greens added for even more savory flavor.

I am a white rice lover. I can't help it. I know I'm supposed to like brown rice. I eat it because it's good for me and I am supposed to, but the truth is that I really prefer white rice. Maybe it's my grandmother's South Carolina blood rolling through my veins. So, with most of my rice recipes, I try to make it healthier in other ways. If you want to use brown rice, you go right ahead.

1 tablespoon pure olive oil

1 sweet onion, chopped

2 stalks celery, chopped

1 poblano chile, cored, seeded, and chopped

3 garlic cloves, very finely chopped

4 ounces chicken livers, finely chopped, or chicken andouille sausage, casings removed and finely chopped

1 cup long-grain white or jasmine brown rice

1 tablespoon chopped fresh thyme

2 teaspoons paprika

1/4 teaspoon cayenne pepper

2 cups water

1 cup coarsely chopped collard greens, finely chopped (about 4 ounces)

Coarse kosher salt and freshly ground black pepper

2 green onions, trimmed and thinly sliced

Hot sauce, for serving

Heat the oil in a large skillet over medium heat. Add the onion, celery, and poblano and cook until soft, 3 to 5 minutes. Add the garlic and cook until fragrant, 45 to 60 seconds. Add the chicken livers and cook until no longer pink, about 3 minutes. Stir in the rice, thyme, paprika, cayenne pepper, the 2 cups water, and chopped collard greens. Season with 1/2 teaspoon of coarse salt and freshly ground black pepper. Cook until the rice is tender, increase the heat to medium-high, and bring to a boil. Cover and decrease the heat to simmer. Cook until the rice is tender, about 18 minutes, or for brown rice, about 35 minutes.

Remove from the heat and let rest, covered, for an additional 5 minutes. No peeking! Add the green onions and fluff with a fork to combine. Taste and adjust for seasoning with salt and pepper. Serve warm with hot sauce on the side.

Calories 194
Fat 4 g
Carbs 33 g
Fiber 3 g
Protein 7 g

BROCCOLI *and* CHEESE "RICE GRITS"

MAKES 7 CUPS TO SERVE 6

Rice "grits" are simply broken grains of rice, a by-product of milling Carolina Gold rice, the fragile long grain rice that's been cultivated on the South Carolina coast for centuries. The broken pieces of rice take on a creamy, risotto-like texture when simmered. This retro-remake is my lightened-up interpretation of the traditional broccoli-rice casserole, without a sodium-laden can of soup in sight.

1 cup long grain white or brown rice or jasmine brown rice

6 cups homemade chicken stock (see note, page 78) or reduced-fat, low-sodium chicken broth

Coarse kosher salt and freshly ground black pepper

1 bay leaf, preferably fresh

1 head broccoli, chopped into florets, stems peeled and thinly sliced

$1/2$ cup freshly grated Parmigiano-Reggiano cheese (about 2 ounces)

$1/2$ teaspoon freshly grated nutmeg

1 tablespoon unsalted butter

Calories 206
Fat 5 g
Carbs 31 g
Fiber 3 g
Protein 11 g

Place the rice in the bowl of a food processor fitted with the metal blade. Pulverize until broken, 3 to 5 minutes. (Rice is astoundingly sturdy.)

In a heavy-bottomed pot, bring the stock and 1 teaspoon of salt to a boil over medium-high heat. Add the pulverized rice and bay leaf; bring to a boil. Decrease the heat to simmer. Cook, stirring occasionally, until the rice is tender, almost like creamy oatmeal or, well, grits, about 20 minutes for white rice and 25 to 30 minutes for brown rice.

Add the broccoli stems and stir to combine. Cook for 1 to 2 minutes, then add the florets and stir to combine. Cook until the broccoli is tender, about 7 minutes. Remove the bay leaf and add the Parmesan, nutmeg, and butter. Taste and adjust for seasoning with salt and pepper.

Ladle into a warmed serving bowl and serve immediately.

HOPPIN' JOHN *and* LIMPIN' SUSAN

MAKES 7 CUPS TO SERVE 8

Hoppin' John, an old-fashioned country dish traditionally served on New Year's Day, is made with peas, rice, and most often flavored with a hunk of pork such as salt pork, fatback, or hog jowl. Legend has it that Limpin' Susan was the wife of Hoppin' John. There seems to be little known about the origin of the name for Limpin' Susan, but the one constant is that it typically consists of rice, bacon, and okra. Both are one-pot, inexpensive meals. In this recipe, I have reunited the happy couple. It seems to me if one is hopping and the other is limping, they probably need each other to lean on. I've lightened things up and reduced the amount of bacon so that it's just a flavoring. You could substitute pure olive oil instead for a completely vegan—and even lighter—dish.

1 strip center-cut bacon, cut into lardons (see note, page 36)

1 sweet onion, chopped

2 cups freshly shelled black-eyed peas (about 1$^{1}/_{2}$ pounds unshelled) or frozen black-eyed peas, thawed

2 cups homemade chicken stock (see note, page 78) or reduced-fat, low-sodium chicken broth, or water

2 cups water

1 dried chile, such as chipotle or ancho, halved and seeded, left whole, or torn into bits for more heat

Coarse kosher salt and freshly ground black pepper

1 cup long grain white rice or jasmine brown rice

8 ounces okra, stemmed and cut into $^{1}/_{2}$-inch pieces

$^{1}/_{4}$ cup chopped fresh parsley

2 green onions, trimmed and chopped

1 small fresh red chile, such as bird's eye or Thai, chopped, for garnish (optional)

Hot sauce

Place a medium pan over medium-high heat. Add the bacon and cook until the fat is rendered, about 3 minutes. Transfer the bacon to a paper towel–lined plate and pour off all but a teaspoon or so of the bacon grease. Return the bacon to the pan. Add the onion and cook until soft and translucent, 3 to 5 minutes. Add peas, stock, the 2 cups water, and the dried chile. Season with salt and pepper. Bring to a boil over high heat, decrease the heat to simmer and cook, uncovered, until the peas are just tender (almost al dente) and about 2 cups of liquid remain, about 20 minutes. Taste and adjust the seasoning with salt and pepper.

Add the rice and okra to the pot, and stir to combine. Cover, and simmer over low heat for about 20 minutes. (If using brown rice, add the rice, but do not add the okra at this point. Let the brown rice simmer for 10 minutes, remove the lid and quickly add the okra. Cover and continue to cook until the rice and okra are tender, an additional 25 minutes.) Do not remove the lid during this part of cooking.

Remove the pot from the heat and allow the rice to steam, still covered, for another 10 minutes. Remove the cover and remove the dried chile. Fluff with a fork; taste and adjust for seasoning with salt and pepper. Scatter the parsley over the top and serve immediately with the green onions, fresh red chile, and hot sauce.

Calories 253
Fat 1 g
Carbs 49 g
Fiber 6 g
Protein 14 g

FARRO *and* CABBAGE

SERVES 6

Farro is one of those "new" grains you've seen on the blogs and in the food magazines. But recent culinary exposure is simply a resurgence in popularity of a very ancient grain. It is toothsome with a slightly nutty taste. One distinct plus with farro is that it doesn't get mushy or rock hard after it's cooked. I will often cook a couple of cups of farro at the beginning of the week and use it in salads or as a side dish, like this one, for the next few days. The cooking time is the same if you decide to double or triple the amount of farro in this recipe.

4 cups water

$^1/_2$ cup semi-pearled farro
(see note, below)

1 teaspoon pure olive oil

1 sweet onion, chopped

2 cloves garlic, finely chopped

$^1/_2$ green cabbage, cored and chopped

Coarse kosher salt and freshly ground black pepper

1 teaspoon chopped fresh thyme

$^1/_4$ teaspoon red pepper flakes

Calories 108
Fat 1 g
Carbs 21 g
Fiber 4 g
Protein 4 g

Bring a medium pot of salted water to a rolling boil over high heat. Add the farro and decrease the heat to simmer. Cook until the farro is tender, about 30 minutes.

Meanwhile, heat the oil in a in a large skillet over medium-high heat. Add the onion and cook until soft and translucent, 3 to 5 minutes. Add the garlic and cook until fragrant, 45 to 60 seconds. Decrease the heat to medium. Add the chopped cabbage and season with salt and pepper. Cook, stirring often, until the cabbage is just tender, 8 to 10 minutes.

Drain the farro and add to the cabbage. Add the thyme and red pepper flakes. Stir to combine and cook for a minute or so until the flavors have combined. Taste and adjust for seasoning with salt and pepper. Serve immediately.

PEARLS OF WISDOM

Keep this in mind if you are new to this grain: whole-grain farro is hulled using a gentler process that leaves the germ and bran intact; it requires overnight soaking before cooking. Look instead for perlato, or, preferably, semi-pearled. Pearling is a process that removes the inedible hull that surrounds the grain. If semi-pearled, some of the germ and bran are removed; if perlato, all are removed. Semi-pearled is quick cooking and has the nutritional germ and bran mostly intact. Even though it is not a complete whole grain, I prefer it for convenience. If your container isn't labeled, just consider that, if your package says it will cook in less than 15 minutes, it's probably pearled; if it takes around 30 minutes, it's probably semi-pearled. And if it takes 60 to 80 minutes, or suggests overnight soaking, it is whole or unpearled.

SOUTHERN STYLE
SHEPHERD'S PIE *with* GRITS

SERVES 8

Nothing nails comfort food like a meaty casserole, as this recipe proves. When someone tells me that they don't like grits, I try to convert the uninitiated with evangelical fervor. If the only grits you've ever had came out of a brown paper packet and were cooked in a microwave with a cup of water, well, those are instant grits and I don't blame you for not liking them. The best grits are stone-ground from whole-grain dried kernels of "dent" corn.

I have altered my basic grits cooking formula to use less water, so that the grits are thick and more appropriate for layering. This rib-sticking dish could also be made ahead and frozen, for great make-ahead meal.

6 cups water

Coarse kosher salt and freshly ground black pepper

1 cup yellow stone-ground grits, fine to medium grind

1 teaspoon pure olive oil

1 sweet onion, chopped

1 celery stalk, chopped

1 carrot, chopped

2 garlic cloves, very finely chopped

1 pound ground chicken

$1/8$ teaspoon red pepper flakes

Pinch of ground cinnamon

Pinch of freshly grated nutmeg

1 (9-ounce) bag baby spinach

$1/4$ cup dry white wine

1 tablespoon chopped fresh oregano

$1/4$ cup plus 1 tablespoon grated Parmigiano-Reggiano cheese (about $2 1/4$ ounces)

Calories 224
Fat 8 g
Carbs 24 g
Fiber 4 g
Protein 15 g

Preheat the oven to 350°F. Spray an 8 by $11 1/2$-inch ovenproof baking dish with nonstick cooking spray; set aside.

In a medium pot over high heat, bring the 6 cups water to a boil. Season with 1 teaspoon coarse salt and pepper. Stir in the grits and return to a boil. Decrease the heat to low, and simmer, stirring often, until thick, about 45 minutes.

Meanwhile, heat the oil in a medium saucepan over medium-high heat. Add the onion, celery, and carrot and cook until soft and starting to color, 3 to 5 minutes. Add the garlic and cook until fragrant, 45 to 60 seconds. Add the chicken and cook, stirring often, until no longer pink, 5 to 7 minutes. Add the red pepper flakes, cinnamon, and nutmeg. Add the spinach and wine. Cover and let wilt, about 2 minutes. Add the oregano and stir to combine. Taste and adjust for seasoning with salt and pepper.

Add $1/4$ cup of the cheese to the grits. Stir to combine and taste and adjust for seasoning with salt and pepper. Cover the bottom of the prepared pan with the chicken mixture. Top with the grits. Using a wet rubber spatula, smooth out the grits over the top of the chicken mixture. Sprinkle over the remaining tablespoon of cheese. Bake until set and golden brown, about 30 minutes. Serve immediately.

TRUE GRIT

White dent corn produces white grits and yellow dent corn produces yellow grits. Grits are further defined by how they are prepared and ground. There are hominy grits, stone-ground grits, and various grades of commercially ground grits.

- Stone-ground grits are made from dried whole corn kernels ground between two stones, just as it has been for centuries. Whole-grain grits are more perishable because they contain the bran and germ and should be refrigerated or frozen. They must also be simmered very slowly for 45 minutes to an hour to coax out their tender, creamy texture. You'll find grits sold under the Anson Mills, McEwen & Sons, and Hoppin John's labels. Bob's Red Mill corn grits are widely available in grocery stores and while the grind is not quite as large, the grits still have their germ and maintain a good corn flavor.

- With large-scale commercially ground grits, the germ and hull are removed to prevent rancidity and improve the product's shelf life. The grits are finely ground and produce a smooth, bland porridge without a whole lot of corn flavor. Also, corn varieties used for artisan stone-ground grits are traditionally left in the field to dry completely, a practice known as field ripening. Commercial milling typically demands that the corn be harvested unripe and dried with forced and sometimes heated, air. Instant grits have the germ and hulls removed and are cooked, then the paste is spread in large sheets. They are then dried and reground. They are virtually a pot of starch with no flavor and very little nutritional value.

- Hominy is made from corn kernels soaked in an alkaline solution of water and lye to remove the kernel's outer hull. When hominy is dried and coarsely ground, the result is hominy grits.

BUTTERMILK POTATO GRATIN

SERVES 8

I would argue that the potato—be it baked or boiled, simmered, or stewed—tops the list of comfort foods *par excellence*. As a matter of fact, there is some honest-to-goodness science that explains our deep desire to feast on spuds. Carbohydrates, in the form of glucose, are the preferred source of energy or fuel for muscle contraction—and potatoes are loaded with carbs. When we're down or feeling poorly, our bodies yearn for our favorite fuel. Once eaten, the carbohydrates break down into smaller sugars that are absorbed and used as energy, fueling muscle contractions. (Any extra eventually gets stored in the body as fat, which is where Americans typically get it wrong because our portions are often too large.)

Here I'm using a well thought-out measure of real butter and a split of full-flavored Gruyère cheese paired with reduced-fat Cheddar to trim down the fat. Lastly, instead of crème fraîche, sour cream, or heavy cream, I'm using low-fat buttermilk for the typical mild tangy taste often found in scalloped potatoes.

1¼ cups 2 percent milk

¾ cup low-fat buttermilk

2 bay leaves, preferably fresh

2 sprigs fresh thyme

1 teaspoon black peppercorns

1 tablespoon unsalted butter

2 tablespoons unbleached all-purpose flour

¼ teaspoon mustard powder

Pinch of cayenne pepper

Coarse kosher salt and freshly ground black pepper

½ cup freshly grated Gruyère cheese (2 ounces)

½ cup freshly grated 75 percent reduced-fat Cheddar cheese (2 ounces)

2 pounds medium Yukon gold potatoes, thinly sliced

Calories 175
Fat 5 g
Carbs 26 g
Fiber 2 g
Protein 8 g

Preheat the oven to 350°F. Spray an 8-inch square ovenproof baking dish with nonstick cooking spray.

In a small saucepan, combine the milk, buttermilk, bay leaves, thyme, and peppercorns. Bring to a gentle simmer over medium-high heat. Remove from the heat and allow to rest and the milks to infuse with flavors for about 5 minutes. (Take that time to slice your potatoes.)

Melt the butter in a medium saucepan over medium heat. Whisk in the flour, and cook until foaming but not browned, about 1 minute. Place a strainer over the saucepan and strain the infused milk into the butter-flour mixture. Whisk to combine. Add the mustard and cayenne, and season with salt and pepper; bring to a boil over high heat. Once it is at a boil, continue cooking, whisking constantly, until the sauce thickens, about 2 minutes. Remove from the heat and add the cheeses. Stir until combined and smooth.

Add the potatoes and stir to combine and coat. Transfer to the prepared baking dish. Cover with aluminum foil and bake for 30 minutes. Remove the foil and continue to bake until bubbly and golden brown, an additional 30 to 45 minutes. Remove to a rack to cool slightly. Serve warm.

MAKEOVER BROCCOLI MAC *and* CHEESE

SERVES 10

From the familiar blue and white box to fancy eight-cheese combinations, Americans can't seem to get enough of mac and cheese. It's rich, simple, and satisfying, friendly and familiar, but never dull. I'll tell you a secret. For years, I didn't have a microwave, but if I felt down in the dumps, my food sin was frozen Stouffer's Macaroni and Cheese. I would go to the store to buy it, remove the pasta Popsicle from the plastic container, transfer it to a baking dish, and bake it in the oven for the suggested hour. I knew how ridiculous it was and that I could have made far better in the same amount of time. Let me just say that macaroni and cheese will make you do crazy things. Instead of making a béchamel, I whisk flour into low-fat milk to make a slurry, and I sub out some of the cheese with low-fat cottage cheese. The end result is that this macaroni makeover is equally creamy and comforting, but without the crazy calories.

1 cup shredded 50 percent reduced-fat extra-sharp Cheddar cheese (4 ounces)

3/4 cup shredded 75 percent reduced-fat extra-sharp Cheddar cheese (3 ounces)

2 tablespoons panko (Japanese) bread crumbs

1/2 teaspoon paprika

1 3/4 cups 2 percent milk

3 tablespoons unbleached all-purpose flour

1 cup low-fat cottage cheese

1/2 teaspoon dry mustard

Pinch freshly grated nutmeg

Coarse kosher salt and freshly ground black pepper

8 ounces (2 cups) whole wheat elbow macaroni

12 ounces (4 cups) broccoli florets and stems

Calories 182
Fat 4 g
Protein 14 g
Carbs 24 g
Fiber 3 g

Preheat oven to 450°F. Bring a large pot of salted water to a boil over high heat. Coat an 8-inch-square (2-quart) baking dish with cooking spray. Combine the two cheeses. Mix 1/4 cup of the cheese mixture, the bread crumbs, and paprika in a small bowl. Set aside.

To make the cheese sauce, heat 1 1/2 cups of the milk in a large heavy saucepan over medium-high heat until simmering. Whisk remaining 1/4 cup milk and the flour in a small bowl until smooth; add to the hot milk and cook, whisking constantly, until the sauce simmers and thickens, 2 to 3 minutes. Remove from heat and stir in the remaining 1 1/2 cups of the cheese mixture and the cottage cheese until melted. Stir in the dry mustard, and nutmeg, and add salt and pepper to taste.

Cook pasta according to package instructions. In the last 3 minutes of cooking, add the broccoli florets. Drain well and add to the cheese sauce; mix well. Spread the pasta-broccoli mixture in the prepared baking dish; sprinkle with the bread crumb mixture. Bake until bubbly and golden brown, about 20 minutes. Remove to a rack to cool slightly. Serve warm.

SWEET POTATO GRATIN
WITH HERB CRUMBLE

SERVES 8

Earthy, rich sweet potatoes are one of fall's most delicious vegetables and pair wonderfully with pecans, one of fall's most delicious nuts. You'll be shocked when you take a bite of this dish. Everyone always assumes they will be hit with a rush of sugar, and yet this sweet potato dish is distinctively full-flavored and savory, a welcome departure from typical marshmallow-topped and bourbon-drenched sweet potato dishes. This recipe utilizes whole wheat pastry flour, which is more nutritionally dense than refined all-purpose flour but also is not as dense and heavy as regular whole wheat flour. Look for Bob's Red Mill whole wheat pastry flour in well-stocked grocery stores. I know Thanksgiving can be tricky. No one wants to give up a favorite dish, but slip this one into the mix and it's certain to become a family favorite.

If you want to take a serious shortcut for this dish, you can substitute one 29-ounce can of pumpkin puree or canned sweet potatoes. The herb-pecan topping tastes equally great with both.

3 large sweet potatoes

1/2 cup coarsely chopped pecans

1/2 cup whole wheat pastry flour, plus more for your hands

2 tablespoons freshly grated Parmigiano-Reggiano cheese

1/2 teaspoon baking powder

1/4 teaspoon fine sea salt, plus more for seasoning

1/4 teaspoon freshly ground black pepper, plus more for seasoning

3 tablespoons 2 percent milk

1 tablespoon pure olive oil

1 tablespoon chopped fresh sage

1 teaspoon firmly packed dark brown sugar

1/8 teaspoon freshly grated nutmeg

Calories 98
Fat 7 g
Carbs 7 g
Fiber 1 g
Protein 2 g

Preheat the oven to 400°F. Line a rimmed baking sheet with a silicone mat or parchment paper. (This will help with cleanup.) Spray a 2-quart shallow baking dish with nonstick cooking spray. Set aside.

Using a fork, pierce the sweet potatoes in several places and place on the prepared baking sheet. Bake until fork-tender, about 50 minutes. Remove to a rack to cool.

When the potatoes are almost tender, prepare the topping: In a small bowl, combine the chopped pecans, flour, Parmesan, baking powder, salt, and pepper. Stir to combine. Add the milk, oil, and sage. Stir until well combined. Set aside.

When the sweet potatoes are cool enough to handle, peel the potatoes, discarding the skin. Place the pulp in large bowl. Add the brown sugar and nutmeg. Season with salt and pepper. Smash the potatoes with a potato masher until chunky.

Transfer the sweet potatoes to the prepared baking dish. Lightly flour your hands and crumble the topping in small, cherry size pieces on top of the sweet potatoes. Transfer to the oven and bake until golden brown, about 30 minutes. Serve immediately.

CHAPTER 5

SEAFOOD *and* SHELLFISH

ACCORDING TO THE USDA, we need to be eating seafood twice a week! Seafood and shellfish are high in protein, low in fat, and the omega-3 fatty acids present in fish are good for your heart. Omega-3 fatty acids are a type of unsaturated fatty acid and research suggests they may reduce inflammation throughout the body. (Inflammation, by the way, can damage your blood vessels and lead to heart disease.) The Mediterranean diet, based on the traditional eating habits of Greece, Spain, and southern Italy, is probably the most famous example of a dietary regimen rich in omega-3 fatty acids and seafood. But, come to think of it, the Mediterranean diet isn't really a diet at all—it's simply an eating lifestyle that emphasizes good-for-you foods like seafood and shellfish, vegetables, beans, nuts, and olive oil. This "diet" proves it's possible to celebrate real food while losing weight and keeping it off.

When I am really hungry, I don't reach for red meat or a pork chop. I actually go for fish. Think about it. Three ounces of mahi mahi, for example, rings up about 93 calories. Three ounces of

top sirloin steak is 158 calories—and is about this size of three fingers. Red meat just doesn't give you as much bang for your buck. Of course, if you've been reading the book up until now, you'll probably say, "But Virginia, the point of eating isn't solely about quantity, I want to eat delicious, satisfying, food!" And you're absolutely right. But hey, sometimes more is more, and I can eat more fish than I can steak.

I've found three reasons that restrict people from cooking fish at home: accessibility, expense, and cooking knowledge. If you are in a larger city, you have access to fresh fish (or at least defrosted frozen fish) at your grocery store whether you are near the coast or not. If you don't see fresh fish at the counter, take a look in the freezer section. There's more to frozen seafood than fish sticks and fried coconut shrimp. Whole Foods Markets sells frozen, vacuum-sealed fish in individual portions. Major grocery stores often sell whole peeled shrimp and fish fillets. The truth is that a great deal of seafood is actually frozen on the boat and later defrosted in the store, so there's no need to automatically assume it's an inferior product. Obviously, fresh is best, but good quality frozen is not only available, it's also often less expensive than fresh.

In terms of cooking knowledge, this chapter contains a variety of recipes with different techniques, but first, you need to hook your fish. Sniff the fish, if possible. There should be no strong odor. Fresh fish smells sweet and clean. Look for a moist surface and firm flesh. Splits or cracks in fillets are signs of drying. Ask the person at the counter to press the fish gently. The indentation should spring back. If not, take a pass. Chefs and seafood experts always examine whole fish when they want to judge freshness. A fresh fish has clear eyes. They're not clouded or sunken. Be dubious of a counter or shop where all whole fish are whole, but headless—not a good sign. Keep fish fresh by burying it in ice. Take a shallow container, cover the bottom with crushed ice or cubes, then put the fish on that and cover with more ice. Cook within a day of purchase.

If you're inexperienced cooking fish, fear not, my friend—the recipes in this chapter are easy and foolproof. I find that it's easier to avoid dry fish when you bake it in the oven, so both Miso-Glazed Catfish with Edamame and Spicy Winter Greens and Lemon-Basil North Georgia Trout are cooked that way. Red Snapper Provençal on Stone-Ground Grits with Parmesan and Herbs and Pan-Seared Fish Steaks with Cherry Tomatoes and Basil are served with a light sauce that will also help prevent the fish from drying out. I'm also sharing a couple of simple yet highly flavorful recipes for shellfish—Beer-Battered Shrimp and Bacon and Chile-Wrapped Scallops. Lastly,

I round it out the chapter with a couple of one-pot meals excellent for a special dinner or a supper club.

As a cook, I am wildly passionate about sustainable seafood. I write about it as often as I can in print, online, and through my blog. I teach sustainable seafood in cooking classes all across the country, and I only buy, cook, and eat sustainable seafood. I do this because I am on the Blue Ribbon Task Force for the Monterey Bay Aquarium and a member of Chefs Collaborative. I "walk what I talk."

According to many scientists and scientific organizations like Seafood Watch, the Marine Stewardship Council, and the Blue Ocean Institute, we are seriously jeopardizing the health and welfare of the oceans. First, we are eating out of the ocean like it is an endless Las Vegas buffet, and it's not. We're also destroying habitats of thriving fisheries through more direct ways such as pollution and runoff. We need to do something sooner rather than later to correct our perilous course. What can you do? Download the Seafood Watch app for your smartphone and use it! Buy only sustainable fish and shellfish and ask for it when you eat out at restaurants as well. Seafood retailers and restaurants play a primary role in the conservation of ocean resources. When you ask businesses to support ocean-friendly seafood, you can help make change happen. Good businesses listen to their customers! Let your community business owners know that sustainable seafood is on your shopping list. It may all seem very overwhelming, but the choices we make, one meal at a time for both the earth and our bodies, add up. Together we can make a difference.

FISH SUBSTITUTIONS

Fish fall easily into three categories: delicate-, medium-, and firm-fleshed. These categories reflect how fish respond to cooking methods and which substitutions work.

Delicate

Treat delicate fish with care when you cook them; use a fish spatula or wide spatula, not tongs or a fork when moving them in the pan. They flake easily and have a soft texture when cooked. These fish are traditionally sold as fillets, and they are best prepared by poaching, braising, pan-frying, or baking.

The following fish can be substituted for one another in recipes:

- sole, flounder, turbot, plaice, flake, sand dabs

Medium

These fish flake easily, but with more resistance than delicate fish, and are firmer when cooked. They are the most versatile fish to cook and can be used when your recipe specifies "or other flaky white fish." They are best prepared by baking, broiling, braising, pan-frying, or grilling.

The following fish can be substituted for one another in recipes:

- farmed arctic char, farmed steelhead trout, farmed rainbow trout, wild salmon

- US mahi mahi, US grouper, monkfish

- US red snapper, Pacific halibut, walleye

- tilapia, bass (freshwater), pike, mid-Atlantic tilefish

Firm

These fish don't flake easily when cooked and have a meaty texture. They are best prepared over high heat—by grilling or sautéing, for example.

The following fish can be substituted for one another in recipes:

- US pompano, Pacific amberjack, US catfish

- troll pole–caught or MSC-certified yellowfin or albacore tuna, US swordfish, farmed sturgeon, Pacific rockfish, Pacific cod, yellow perch, sablefish

RED SNAPPER PROVENÇAL
ON STONE-GROUND GRITS WITH PARMESAN AND HERBS

SERVES 6

Red snapper is a Gulf favorite. I remember my parents going deep-sea fishing when I was a child and returning with massive coolers packed with red snapper. I absolutely love the ocean. It's so intensely primal and the only feeling that would remotely come close would be the basic human reaction to fire. I'm pretty certain that if I lived at the beach I'd ditch my red lipstick pretty darn quick and become someone who fishes a whole lot more and bathes a little less. Fish and grits is an old-timey country dish that might be enjoyed for both breakfast or supper. Here I've gussied it up with fennel and olives. This is a family favorite.

GRITS

1 tablespoon pure olive oil

1 sweet onion, grated

2 cups 2 percent milk

2 cups water

Coarse kosher salt and freshly ground black pepper

1 cup stone-ground grits

1 tablespoon unsalted butter

$^1/_2$ cup grated Parmigiano-Reggiano cheese (about 2 ounces)

1 tablespoon chopped fresh flat-leaf parsley

To make the grits, in a heavy-bottomed saucepan, heat the oil over medium heat. Add the onion and cook until transparent, about 3 minutes. Add the milk, water, and 1 teaspoon of salt. Bring the mixture to a boil over high heat. Whisk in the grits, decrease the heat to low, and simmer, whisking occasionally, until the grits are creamy and thick, 45 to 60 minutes. Stir in the butter, cheese, and parsley. Taste, adjust for seasoning with salt and pepper, and keep warm.

Preheat the oven to 375°F. Brush a shallow, ovenproof casserole with some of the oil for the fish; set aside.

To make the sauce for the fish, heat the remaining 1 tablespoon oil in a large skillet over medium-high heat. Add the fennel and cook until just tender, 5 to 7 minutes. Add the onion and cook until soft and translucent, 2 to 3 minutes. Add the garlic and chopped thyme and cook until fragrant, 45 to 60 seconds. Add the tomatoes and sauté until soft, 5 to 7 minutes. Add the olives and vinegar. Taste and adjust for seasoning with salt and pepper.

CONTINUED

RED SNAPPER

1 tablespoon olive oil, plus more
for the pan

1 small bulb fennel, cored and diced,
fronds reserved for garnish

1 sweet onion, diced

3 large garlic cloves, finely chopped

1 tablespoon chopped fresh thyme,
plus thyme sprigs for garnish

2 tomatoes, cored, seeded, and
chopped, or 1 (14.5-ounce) can
no-salt-added diced tomatoes

20 kalamata or other brine-cured
black olives, halved and pitted

1 tablespoon red wine vinegar

Coarse kosher salt and freshly
ground black pepper

6 (4-ounce) red snapper fillets,
skinned

Calories 405
Fat 19 g
Carbs 43 g
Fiber 4 g
Protein 17 g

To cook the fish, place the snapper in the prepared casserole; season
with salt and pepper. Spoon the sauce over the fillets. Bake until
opaque in the center when pierced with the tip of a knife, about
10 minutes.

To serve, place a spoonful of the grits in individual shallow bowls.
Top with a portion of the fish and ladle over some of the tomato
sauce. Garnish with sprigs of thyme and fennel fronds.

GRITS BASICS

When cooking grits for eating on their own for breakfast or
as a side dish, use a ratio of 4 cups liquid to 1 cup whole-grain,
stone-ground grits. I most often use a combination of water and
2 percent milk, but you can also use all water, a combination of
water and stock, or stock and milk. Some recipes use all milk, half
and half, or heavy cream, but I think they overpower the subtlety of
the corn flavor—and have no place in a lightened up way of eating.

LEMON-BASIL NORTH GEORGIA TROUT

SERVES 4

I have always, always loved to fish. Mama tells me that I caught my first fish when I was so young, that in my excitement, I jumped out of my diaper. There's nothing like fishing to me for relaxation and enjoying nature. If you are new to cooking fish or worried about overcooking, this recipe has "training wheels." The spicy-herb topping helps protect the fish in the heat of the hot oven and can help prevent it from drying out and overcooking. This trout would be lovely served with freshly sliced tomato on a bed of crispy greens.

8 large leaves chopped fresh basil

8 sprigs chopped fresh flat-leaf parsley

4 small cloves garlic, very finely chopped

1 teaspoon red pepper flakes, or to taste

Finely grated zest of 1 lemon

1 tablespoon extra-virgin olive oil

2 (8-ounce) trout fillets, halved

Coarse kosher salt

Calories 97
Fat 6 g
Carbs 1 g
Fiber .3 g
Protein 9 g

Preheat the oven to 450°F. Line a rimmed baking sheet with a nonstick silicone baking mat.

Combine the basil, parsley, garlic, red pepper flakes, and lemon zest in a small bowl. Brush each piece of fish with some of the oil, season with salt, then dust the top side with the herb mixture. Place the fish on the prepared baking sheet and bake until the fish is opaque, 5 to 7 minutes. Serve immediately on warmed serving plates.

PAN-SEARED FISH STEAKS
WITH CHERRY TOMATOES AND BASIL

SERVES 4

Pepper is one of my favorite spices. I really like to use it with purposeful intent, as with this dish where it's the main accent flavor. The size of the grind and the blend of peppercorns can make a difference in the end result, so I'm suggesting a blend of peppercorns. However, if you are in a pinch with your pepper, you can also use a mill and simply adjust the setting so the pepper is very coarsely cracked.

Hearty, firm-fleshed fish on the bone is best for this dish. Look for Pacific halibut, wild salmon, or sustainable swordfish steaks. Steaks are pieces of fish cut in cross section that generally still have skin and sometimes a bone in the center, depending on the size of the fish. A fish fillet is simply a boneless piece of fish. If you are using a fillet, make sure to pepper the flesh side, not the skin side of the fish, or remove the skin all together.

1 tablespoon mixed white and black peppercorns

Coarse kosher salt

1 tablespoon pure olive oil

4 (4-ounce) swordfish, halibut, or salmon steaks, cut 1-inch thick

20 cherry tomatoes

1 cup lightly packed whole fresh basil leaves

Orange or lemon wedges, for accompaniment

Calories 193
Fat 10 g
Carbs 4 g
Fiber 1 g
Protein 21 g

Preheat the oven to 350°F. Crush the peppercorns using the bottom of a heavy skillet on a clean work surface or pulse in a spice grinder until just cracked. Set aside. Sift to remove the finest particles of pepper. (They can make the fish far too hot.)

Season both sides of the steak with salt. Rub one side of the steaks with the pepper. Heat the tablespoon of oil in a 12-inch heavy-duty ovenproof skillet over medium-high heat until shimmering. Add the fish steaks, pepper-side down, and cook, without moving, until a crust has formed, 3 to 4 minutes. Using a spatula, turn the steaks and scatter over the tomatoes and basil leaves. Transfer to the oven and cook until the fish is firm, about 4 additional minutes. Remove the skillet to a rack to cool slightly and let the fish set. Serve immediately with orange or lemon wedges on the side.

PICK A PINT OF PICKLED PEPPER

Pepper berries grow in clusters and are dried and processed to produce three types of peppercorns—black, white, and green, all from the same plant. The most common is the black peppercorn. The less pungent white peppercorn has been allowed to ripen, after which the skin is removed and the berry is dried. Green peppercorns are the unripe, immature berries of the same plant.

MISO-GLAZED CATFISH
WITH EDAMAME AND SPICY WINTER GREENS

SERVES 4

You might be thinking, "What on earth is miso doing in a Southern cookbook?" To that I say the South is a far less homogeneous place than it once was. And, when conceiving this recipe, all I could think about was the umami of the miso and how that would mimic the smoky salty flavors of Southern-style country ham. It's a perfect match. I've added shelled edamame for a great, fresh, and protein-packed bit of crunch.

1 tablespoon canola oil, plus more for the baking dish

1 pound thin catfish fillets, or 4 (4-ounce) catfish fillets

Freshly ground black pepper

4 tablespoons low-sodium miso paste

4 cups water

8 cups chopped winter greens, such as kale or collards (about 8 ounces)

2 cups shelled edamame, thawed if frozen

1 sweet onion, thinly sliced

1 jalapeño chile, sliced, or to taste

1/2 teaspoon red pepper flakes

Calories 237
Fat 8 g
Carbs 23 g
Fiber 8 g
Protein 18 g

Preheat the oven to broil and position a rack about 5 inches from the heat. Brush a medium baking dish with oil.

Place the catfish in the greased baking dish. Heartily season the fillets with freshly ground black pepper. Using a spatula, thinly spread 1 tablespoon of the miso on the tops of the fillets. Set aside.

In a large saucepan over high heat, combine the remaining 3 tablespoons of miso with the 4 cups of water. Bring to a boil. Add the winter greens, edamame, onion, jalapeño, and red pepper flakes. Season with freshly ground black pepper. Decrease the heat to simmer. Cook until the vegetables are tender, about 10 minutes.

Place the miso-glazed catfish under the broiler. Cook until the fish is opaque and the miso is deep golden brown, 8 to 10 minutes, depending on the strength of your broiler.

To serve, spoon the vegetables in equal portions into warmed shallow bowls. Place a portion of catfish on top. Spoon over some of the miso broth used to cook the vegetables. Serve immediately.

WHAT A CATCH!

A specialty of the South, catfish is the leading aquaculture-produced seafood product in the United States. What does "aquaculture" mean? Well, think aqua plus agriculture; it's the word used to define farming fish and shellfish. Farm-raised domestic catfish has been on the top ten list of most frequently consumed seafood products in the United States for almost twenty years. Make sure to look for US farm-raised catfish instead of imports like basa or swai, which are less likely to be sustainably raised.

CITRUS-GRILLED SHRIMP
WITH BLOODY MARY COCKTAIL SAUCE

MAKES 6 SKEWERS AND 1 CUP SAUCE

Shrimp are a fantastic lean protein and very quick to cook, so they're pretty much the best "fast" food you can eat! To butterfly shrimp, cut them with a sharp paring knife along the back; discard the veins, and open up the shrimp, butterfly-style. I'm using a wee bit of food science to enhance the flavor of the cocktail sauce. Tomatoes contain alcohol-soluble flavors that can only be delivered to your taste receptors in the presence of alcohol. The vodka combined with the ketchup makes this basic recipe shine. Leave the peel on the citrus so it won't fall apart on the grill.

SHRIMP

1 grapefruit, halved

1 orange, halved

1 garlic clove, mashed to a paste with salt (see note, page 113)

1 pound jumbo (18/20 count) shrimp, shelled, tails intact, butterflied, and deveined

Coarse kosher salt and freshly ground black pepper

2 stalks celery, cut into 1-inch pieces

BLOODY MARY COCKTAIL SAUCE

Grated zest and juice of 1 lemon

$1/2$ cup low-sodium ketchup

1 tablespoon freshly grated horseradish

1 tablespoon vodka

2 teaspoons reduced-sodium Worcestershire sauce

Pinch celery salt

Hot sauce

Freshly ground black pepper

To prepare the shrimp, squeeze the juice from one grapefruit half and one orange half into a large bowl. Add the shrimp and season with salt and pepper. Toss the shrimp to combine and coat. Cover and refrigerate to marinate for about 30 minutes.

Meanwhile, make the cocktail sauce. In a small bowl, combine the lemon zest and juice, ketchup, horseradish, vodka, Worcestershire, and celery salt, and season to taste with hot sauce, and pepper. Stir until well combined; set aside.

Prepare a medium-hot charcoal fire as directed on page 23. Or preheat a gas grill to high or a grill pan over high heat.

Cut the remaining grapefruit and orange halves into 1-inch pieces. (You will probably have more than you need.) Skewer the shrimp without packing them too tight, inserting a piece of citrus and celery between every few shrimp. Grill the shrimp, turning once, until charred on both sides and just cooked through, 5 minutes total. Serve immediately with the cocktail sauce.

SIZE MATTERS

Jumbo, large, and medium are all arbitrary designations when it comes to shrimp. Chefs purchase shrimp according to the count per pound: 21/25 count shrimp indicates that there are between 21 and 25 shrimp per pound. Regardless of size, when buying shrimp, make sure they smell mildly sweet. If there is any scent of ammonia or fishy smell, it's a sign the shrimp are no longer fresh.

Grilled Shrimp
Calories 66
Fat .2 g
Carbs 5 g
Fiber .6 g
Protein 12 g

Bloody Mary Cocktail Sauce per tablespoon
Calories 14
Fat .1 g
Carbs 3 g
Fiber .2 g
Protein .2 g

BEER-BATTERED SHRIMP
WITH SPICY KETCHUP

SERVES 4 | MAKES 1½ CUPS SPICY KETCHUP

Fried shrimp might seem a thing of the past if you are trying to eat healthy. These are still a special treat, but are pan-fried, not deep fried, and super crispy because they are made with beer. The alcohol in the beer evaporates quickly as the shrimp cooks leaving them extra crispy. I know it might seem silly to make your own ketchup, and yes, on many busy days homemade ketchup will be too much work. But this zippy sauce is made from wholesome ingredients— no fillers, stabilizers, or corn syrup—and will last up to four weeks in the refrigerator. Make a batch and put it in mason jar for some amped-up flavor.

SPICY KETCHUP

1 tablespoon pure olive oil

1 sweet onion, grated

1 garlic clove, mashed to a paste with salt (see note, below)

1 (14.5-ounce) no-salt-added canned tomatoes with juice, pureed

1 tablespoon tomato paste

¼ cup sherry vinegar

1 tablespoon honey

1 tablespoon smoked hot paprika

Coarse kosher salt and freshly ground black pepper

Spicy Ketchup per tablespoon
Calories 18
Fat .6 g
Carbs 3 g
Fiber .4 g
Protein .3 g

To make the ketchup, heat the olive oil in a large pot over medium heat. Add the onion and cook, stirring, until softened, about 8 minutes. Add the garlic and cook until fragrant, 45 to 60 seconds. Add the tomatoes, tomato paste, sherry vinegar, honey, and smoked paprika, then season with salt. Cook until thickened, 45 to 60 minutes.

To prepare the shrimp, combine the panko and cilantro in a shallow baking dish and stir to combine. Combine the rice flour, unbleached all-purpose flour, and baking soda in a large bowl, stirring with a whisk. Gradually add the beer, stirring with a whisk until a smooth batter.

CONTINUED

GARLIC PASTE

To prepare garlic paste, place the broad side of an unpeeled clove of garlic on a clean work surface. Give it a whack with the side of a chef's knife. Remove the outside papery skin, and using the knife, trim the tough basal plane at the top of the clove. Halve the clove lengthwise and remove the green shoot, if present, as it is bitter. Coarsely chop the garlic, then sprinkle it with coarse salt. (The salt acts as an abrasive and helps chop the garlic.) Then, using the flat side of the chef's knife like a palette knife, press firmly on the garlic, crushing a little at a time. Repeat until the garlic is a smooth paste.

SHRIMP

$^1/_2$ cup panko (Japanese) bread crumbs

1 tablespoon chopped fresh cilantro leaves

$^2/_3$ cup rice flour or cornstarch

$^1/_2$ cup unbleached all-purpose flour

$^1/_2$ teaspoon baking soda

4 ounces light beer

6 tablespoons canola oil

1 pound large (21/25 count) shrimp, peeled and deveined

1 lemon, thinly sliced

Coarse kosher salt and freshly ground black pepper

Shrimp
Calories 279
Fat 11 g
Carbs 19 g
Fiber 1 g
Protein 24 g

Line a plate with paper towels. Heat a large nonstick skillet over medium-high heat. Add 3 tablespoons of the canola oil to pan; swirl to coat. Working one at a time and using the tail as a handle, dip the shrimp in the batter and shake off the excess. Dredge the shrimp in the panko mixture, making sure to coat both sides. Place the shrimp in a single layer in the pan, and cook until golden brown, about 2$^1/_2$ minutes on each side. Remove the shrimp from pan; drain on paper towels. Repeat with the remaining oil, shrimp, batter, and panko mixture. At the end of cooking, sear the lemon slices in the hot oil until slightly charred.

Serve the shrimp and lemon slices hot with the spicy ketchup.

SHORE THING

Summer vacations often are spent at the beach. There's nothing like a deep-fried fisherman's platter to send your healthy eating plan overboard! If you're deep-sea dining, look for healthier choices like peel-and-eat shrimp, steamed lobster, and broiled or grilled fish fillet. Toss the tartar sauce and ask for cocktail sauce or a simple squeeze of lemon instead.

BACON *and* CHILE-WRAPPED SCALLOPS
WITH LEMON GREMOLATA

SERVES 4

Bacon-wrapped scallops are a classic combination of sea and salt. Sadly, they all too often become overcooked and greasy. To achieve crispy bacon, tender scallops, and a star-studded supper, use a proper amount of bacon. You don't need a whole slice of bacon to wrap around a scallop. In this recipe, the bacon is cut into four strips so it's simply a stripe around the shellfish. The bacon is also parcooked, eliminating some of the fat and grease.

Gremolata is a traditional condiment served with veal osso bucco, to cut the richness of that dish. It also gives a nice citrusy kick to fish and shellfish dishes.

GREMOLATA

¼ cup chopped fresh flat-leaf parsley

1 tablespoon chopped fresh thyme

2 cloves garlic, very finely chopped

Finely grated zest and juice of 1 lemon

2 tablespoons extra-virgin olive oil

Coarse kosher salt and freshly ground black pepper

SCALLOPS

3 slices center-cut bacon

16 large sea scallops (about 1½ pounds)

Coarse kosher salt and freshly ground black pepper

1 banana or Hungarian wax pepper or small poblano chile, cored and sliced into ¼-inch-thick rings

---

Calories 253
Fat 11 g
Carbs 7 g
Fiber 1 g
Protein 31 g

Adjust an oven rack to 6 inches from the heat and preheat the broiler to high. Line a rimmed baking sheet with a silicone mat or parchment paper.

To make the gremolata, combine the parsley, thyme, garlic, lemon zest and juice, and olive oil in a small bowl. Season with salt and pepper. Set aside.

To make the scallops, slice each piece of bacon lengthwise into two, long thin strips, then cut each strip into half vertically to create 4 smaller pieces per slice (you should have a total of 12 bacon pieces). Spread the bacon pieces out over two layers of paper towels on a microwave-safe plate, then cover with two more layers of paper towels. Microwave on high until the bacon fat begins to melt but the bacon is still pliable, 1 to 2 minutes, depending on the strength of your microwave.

Meanwhile, put the scallops in a bowl. Season with salt and pepper.

Wrap a piece of the microwaved bacon around 12 of the scallops and place on the prepared baking sheet. Fit the 4 remaining scallops in the center of 4 of the rings of pepper. Scatter the remaining rings on the baking sheet. Broil until the scallops are firm and the edges of the bacon are brown, about 5 minutes, depending on the strength of your broiler.

Serve 3 bacon-wrapped and 1 chile-wrapped scallop per person, topped with the gremolata.

SALMON PATTIES
WITH LEMON-CAPER SAUCE

MAKES FOUR 4-OUNCE PATTIES | MAKES ABOUT ¹/₂ CUP SAUCE

Dede, my grandfather, loved green beans, and grew bushels of them in his massive garden. When he and my grandmother traveled in their motor home all across the country, they would take cases of home-canned green beans to eat. They would often journey to Alaska—from Georgia—to go salmon fishing. Weeks later, when they arrived in Alaska, they would fish for salmon in the cold, racing rivers and my grandmother would can the salmon, using her pressure cooker, in the now-empty jars that once held green beans. I was in college before I ever tried commercially canned salmon.

Traditional salmon patties or croquettes are often made with canned salmon and skillet fried. These are made with fresh salmon and baked, for a fresh and light alterative that is perfect with an arugula salad or on a bun. Salmon is a great starter fish if you aren't all that familiar with cooking seafood (it is widely available), and from a nutrition standpoint, it is packed with omega-3 and omega-6 fatty acids. Make sure to search out wild-caught salmon, such as wild-caught Alaska salmon that is considered a "Best Choice" by Seafood Watch and certified as sustainable by the standards of the Marine Stewardship Council.

LEMON-CAPER SAUCE

1 lemon

1 tablespoon chopped onion

1 tablespoon Dijon mustard

1 tablespoon capers, drained and finely chopped

¹/₂ celery stalk, very finely chopped

Coarse kosher salt and freshly ground black pepper

2 tablespoons extra-virgin olive oil

Lemon Caper Sauce per tablespoon
Calories 37
Fat 4 g
Carbs 1 g
Fiber .3 g
Protein .1 g

To make the sauce, zest the lemon with a handheld grater and reserve the zest for the salmon. To section the lemon, using a small sharp knife and a cutting board, slice off the top and bottom so the lemon will stand upright. To section the lemon, set the fruit upright on the board. Working from top to bottom, slice off the peel, white pith, and outer membranes from the lemon to expose the segments. Carefully cut each segment away from its membranes and put in a bowl along with any juice. Squeeze any remaining juice from the membranes, then discard. Add the onion, mustard, capers, and celery. Whisk until combined. Season with salt and pepper. Whisk in the olive oil in a slow steady stream. Taste and adjust for seasoning with salt and pepper.

SALMON

1/2 onion, finely chopped

1/2 stalk celery, finely chopped

10 ounces boneless, skinless salmon fillet, pin bones removed, and cut into 1/4-inch dice

1 cups fresh whole wheat bread crumbs or whole wheat panko (Japanese) bread crumbs

1 large egg

1 garlic clove, finely chopped

1 tablespoon chopped fresh flat-leaf parsley

1 teaspoon Dijon mustard

Pinch cayenne pepper

Coarse kosher salt and freshly ground black pepper

———————

Salmon Patty
Calories 220
Fat 11 g
Carbs 21 g
Fiber 3 g
Protein 11 g

To make the salmon, preheat the oven to 450°F. Line a rimmed baking sheet with a silicone mat. Place the onion and celery in a microwave-safe bowl and cook until softened, about 3 minutes. Set aside to cool slightly.

In a large bowl, combine the salmon, bread crumbs, egg, onion mixture, garlic, parsley, mustard, reserved lemon zest, and cayenne pepper. Season with salt and pepper. (Simply microwave a teaspoon or so until the salmon is cooked so you can taste and adjust for seasoning.) Using a large ice cream scoop or 1/2 cup measure, shape the salmon mixture with your hands into 4 cakes and place on the prepared baking sheet. Bake 5 minutes, then, using an offset spatula or batter turner, flip and bake an additional 5 minutes.

Serve immediately with the sauce.

GULF COAST SEAFOOD STEW

SERVES 8

Before modern transportation and refrigeration, seafood was a luxury to people who lived in inland Southern states. But it was so prevalent in the coastal states that it was essentially poor people's food there—hard to believe, considering how expensive most seafood is nowadays. This stew was inspired by poor man's dishes like gumbo in Louisiana and Frogmore stew in the Low Country.

4 cups homemade chicken stock (see note, page 78) or reduced-fat, low-sodium chicken broth

3/4 pound unpeeled, large (21/25 count) raw shrimp

1 stalk celery

1 large sweet onion

1 poblano chile

1 tablespoon pure olive oil

2 garlic cloves, chopped

1 teaspoon Homemade Creole Seasoning (page 135)

1 tablespoon fresh thyme leaves

1 bay leaf, preferably fresh

1 (12-ounce) bottle light beer

6 ounces chicken or turkey andouille sausage, cut into 1/2-inch pieces

1/2 pound small red potatoes, halved

3/4 pound fresh white fish fillets, (such as snapper, grouper, or catfish), cubed

Coarse kosher salt and freshly ground black pepper

Calories 185
Fat 5 g
Carbs 11 g
Fiber 2 g
Protein 22 g

Place the chicken stock in a medium saucepan. Peel the shrimp and add the shells to the chicken stock. Refrigerate the shrimp in an airtight container until you need them. Bring the chicken stock to a boil over medium-high heat then decrease the heat to simmer.

Chop the celery, onion, and chile, reserving the celery ends and onion peel. Set aside. Add the onion peel and celery ends (but not the chile trimmings) to the pot of simmering chicken stock. (Using the leftover bits will layer the flavor and will result in a very flavorful broth; if you don't have time, it's okay to ignore this advice.) Let the mixture simmer until the shrimp shells are bright pink and the broth is well-flavored, about 8 to 10 minutes.

Heat the oil in a large pot over medium-high heat. Add the reserved celery, onion, and chile and cook until soft and the onion is translucent, 3 to 5 minutes. Add the garlic and cook until fragrant, 45 to 60 seconds. Add the Creole seasoning, thyme, bay leaf, beer, andouille, and potatoes. Strain the chicken stock over, discarding the shells and vegetable peels. Bring to a boil over high heat, then decrease the heat to simmer. Cook, stirring occasionally and skimming any fat from the surface, until the potatoes are tender, about 30 minutes.

Add the fish and cook gently until just opaque, 3 to 4 minutes. Add the shrimp, and cook until the shrimp are pink, an additional 3 to 4 minutes. Taste the broth and adjust for seasoning with salt and pepper.

To serve, transfer portions of the seafood to warmed shallow soup bowls. Spoon the broth over the seafood and serve immediately.

SMOKY SEAFOOD ÉTOUFÉE

SERVES 4

Growing up in Louisiana had enormous impact on my childhood culinary experience. Mama didn't know anyone when we first moved there, so she immersed herself in the cuisine to learn the culture. She bought copies of Junior League cookbooks bound in plastic ring binders. My sister and I grew up eating étoufée, gumbo, and jambalaya—and learned how to suck crawfish heads just like a native.

Perhaps the best part of this recipe is that it can be a weeknight supper in less than 30 minutes. *Laissez les bons temps rouler!*

1 tablespoon pure olive oil

2 tablespoons unbleached all-purpose flour

1 sweet onion, chopped

1 stalk celery, diced

1 small green bell pepper, diced

3 cloves garlic, finely chopped

1 tablespoon tomato paste

3/4 cup homemade chicken stock (see note, page 78) or reduced-fat, low-sodium chicken broth

1 pound large shrimp (21/25 count), shelled and deveined

2 tablespoons chopped fresh flat-leaf parsley

1/2 teaspoon smoked paprika

1/4 teaspoon cayenne pepper

Coarse kosher salt and freshly ground black pepper

Cooked long grain white or jasmine brown rice, for accompaniment

2 green onions, trimmed and chopped

Heat the oil in a large skillet over medium-high heat. Add the flour and cook, stirring often, until the roux is pale brown, about 10 minutes. Add the onion, celery, and bell pepper. Cook until the onion is soft and translucent, 3 to 5 minutes. Add the garlic and cook until fragrant, 45 to 60 seconds.

In small bowl, combine the tomato paste and stock. Add the stock mixture to the skillet and bring to a boil, stirring constantly. Decrease the heat to medium and simmer until slightly thickened and the flavors have married, about 10 minutes.

Add the shrimp, parsley, smoked paprika, and cayenne pepper. Cook until heated through, about 5 minutes. Taste and adjust for seasoning with salt and pepper. Spoon over hot rice, garnish with green onions, and serve immediately.

Smoky Seafood Etoufée
(without rice)
Calories 178
Fat 4 g
Carbs 14 g
Fiber 2 g
Protein 22 g

CHAPTER 6

POULTRY

FRIED CHICKEN IS AS SOUTHERN as sweet tea and kudzu. It is so iconic, in fact, that it's nearly become a stereotype. Fried chicken was once called "gospel bird" because it was most often served once a week on Sundays. Meaning, of course, that it was a special occasion meal and there weren't fried chicken drive-through lanes on every other corner. Fried chicken was special. Fried chicken was homemade, so don't waste calories on inadequate fast-food fried chicken.

But this is a book all about lightening up, y'all, so it's time to move beyond our deep-fried inclinations. Chicken and turkey are both very versatile and can be grilled, slow-cooked, baked, sautéed, or roasted. The tips and techniques in this chapter will teach you ways to avoid dry boneless, skinless chicken breasts, how to get the most out of quick-cooking cutlets, and what to do—besides adding eggs, bacon, or bread crumbs—to succeed with ground chicken and poultry.

I'm combating the pall of parched poultry by brining the bird in recipes like Sweet Tea–Brined Turkey Tenderloin or serving it in a sauce with Basil-Peach Chicken Breasts and Spicy Creole Turkey Cutlets with Holy Trinity Tomato Gravy. Lean ground poultry is augmented with savory mushrooms for moisture in Turkey Meatloaf

with Mushroom Gravy and tender, sweet apples in Chicken, Apple, and Cheddar Burgers. I close the coop with a savory recipe for Honey Mustard Carolina Quail. Regardless of what you bird you choose, you'll find plenty of healthy eating choices.

The choices you make in the grocery store are as important as the choices you make in the kitchen, so pay attention to the kind of poultry you buy. You say, "Oh, I don't buy chicken raised with antibiotics or hormones." That's a great start—but it doesn't mean as much as you think it might. The truth is, *all chicken* is hormone-free. USDA regulations prohibit poultry growers from giving hormones or steroids to their birds, so a label saying no hormones is a bit deceiving. It implies some chicken might contain hormones. What about antibiotics? Antibiotics are necessary to control and prevent illness in massive chicken houses. The trouble is, some poultry that is labeled antibiotic free only means the chickens themselves haven't been given antibiotics. It doesn't mean the chicken feed doesn't contain antibiotics, or that they weren't administered to eggs *before* the chicks hatched.

"Free range" is mostly a marketing term. Producers of free-range chickens must simply be able to demonstrate that the poultry has been allowed access to the outside. This does not necessarily mean the chickens are pecking away in a pasture. It only means they have access to the outdoors—and that very well might be a doggie door. The best and most humane choice is always pastured poultry, which means the birds are literally running around in a pasture—but this choice is prohibitively expensive for many people. There are lots of choices and you have to decide what's the most important for you and your family.

I prefer to buy USDA organic chicken; organic chicken is the only chicken that is both hormone and antibiotic free. I sometimes splurge on a bird from my friend Will Harris III, of White Oak Pastures, Bluffton, Georgia, who sells his pastured birds online and at Whole Foods Market locations in the Southeast. Will is a fourth-generation cattleman. Will's ancestor founded White Oak Pastures in south Georgia in the late 1800s after returning home from the Civil War, and the Harris family has raised livestock on the same farm for nearly one hundred fifty years. White Oak Pastures is now the largest organic farm in the state of Georgia, offering grass-fed beef and lamb, free-range pastured poultry, as well as free-range eggs and organic produce. Both the cattle and poultry abattoirs are directly across the street from his family home where he lives with his wife of thirty-five years, Yvonne (or "Von"), and where they raised their three daughters—Jessica, Jenni, and Jodi. It's as beautiful as any part of the country as I have ever seen and reminds me of my childhood. And, the simplicity, honesty, and commitment to doing what is right and good is bedrock to what is best about our country.

Take the time to prepare something thoughtful, healthful, and tasty. Once you taste my Oven-Fried Chicken on a Stick with Vidalia–Honey Mustard Dipping Sauce, I promise, you'll be singing the praises of the gospel bird once again.

IT'S THIGH TIME FOR A NIP AND TUCK

Chicken thighs are likely to be more moist and juicy than boneless, skinless chicken breasts because they are higher in fat. You can substitute thighs for breasts in most recipes, and here are a couple of hints to lighten up your thighs: Make sure to trim away any visible fat or skin left on the thighs when you remove them from the package. And, without the bone the thighs will spread out a bit. Tuck the loose ends under and start the cooking smooth side up so they maintain a better shape.

SMOTHERED *and* COVERED CHICKEN
AND GRAVY

SERVES 4

As a French-trained chef, I adore the concept of the five French mother sauces, which classifies hundreds of sauces into a mere five categories: béchamel, velouté, brown or espagnole, hollandaise, and tomato. Velouté is the closest to Southern gravy and is made by whisking white stock into a roux made from flour and fat. (Technically, the stock has also been used to cook the meat.) However, I'm pretty sure "smothered and covered" doesn't sound nearly as snappy in French. To lighten things up, I am using the merest amount of flour possible and boneless and skinless chicken thighs, and pan-searing, not frying, the meat. This is old-style cooking that is more down-home diner than dinner party, and great for a simple and inexpensive weeknight supper.

2 tablespoons unbleached
all-purpose flour

1 teaspoon onion powder

1 teaspoon smoked paprika

¼ teaspoon cayenne pepper

Coarse kosher salt and freshly
ground black pepper

1 tablespoon canola oil

4 boneless, skinless chicken thighs
(1¼ pounds)

2 sweet onions, sliced

2 garlic cloves, very finely chopped

1 cup homemade chicken stock
(see note, page 78) or reduced-fat,
low-sodium chicken broth, warmed

2 sprigs fresh thyme

1 bay leaf, preferably fresh

Calories 281
Fat 12 g
Carbs 17 g
Fiber 2 g
Protein 26 g

Preheat the oven to 350°F. Combine the flour, onion powder, paprika, and cayenne pepper in a shallow dish. Season with salt and pepper and stir to combine.

Heat the oil in a large ovenproof skillet over medium-high heat until shimmering. Pat the thighs dry and place in the flour-spice mixture to coat on both sides. Shake off the excess. Add the coated thighs to the pan and sear until brown, 1 to 2 minutes per side. Remove to a plate.

To the residual oil, add the onions and decrease the heat to medium. Season with salt and pepper. Cook, stirring occasionally, until the onions are golden brown, 5 to 7 minutes. Add garlic and cook until fragrant, 45 to 60 seconds. Tip the remaining flour-spice mixture into the onions and stir to coat and combine. Add the chicken stock and increase the heat to medium-high. Bring to a boil. Decrease the heat to simmer. Add the reserved chicken thighs with any accumulated juices, the thyme leaves, and bay leaf. Nestle the thighs into the onions and turn to coat. Transfer the skillet to the oven and cook until the juices run clear when pierced with a knife and the temperature reads 165°F when measured with an instant-read thermometer, 20 to 25 minutes. Taste and adjust for seasoning with salt and pepper. Serve immediately.

OVEN-FRIED CHICKEN-ON-A-STICK
WITH VIDALIA-HONEY MUSTARD DIPPING SAUCE

MAKES 16 TO SERVE 8

Who doesn't like food on a stick? There's something naturally fun about handheld food. It elicits memories of country fairs and football games. This recipe was inspired by the offerings of a gas station in Oxford, Mississippi. I am a member of the Southern Foodways Alliance, an organization based out of Ole Miss (the University of Mississippi, to the rest of you) that documents, studies, and celebrates the diverse food cultures of the changing American South. I generally pay a visit to Oxford each fall for the yearly SFA symposium. Being a Southern college town, there are robust opportunities for boozy carousing. Fried-chicken-on-a-stick is food consumed late at night in attempts to mitigate hangovers or the next morning as an answer to one. This recipe maintains the crispy flavor without the calories.

1 tablespoon coarse kosher salt

2 teaspoons paprika

1 teaspoon onion powder

1 teaspoon garlic powder

1 cup low-fat buttermilk

3 boneless, skinless chicken breasts, trimmed (1½ pounds)

2 cups panko (Japanese) bread crumbs

2 tablespoons canola oil

2 large egg whites

1 tablespoon Dijon mustard

Freshly ground black pepper

Vidalia–Honey Mustard Dipping Sauce, for serving (recipe follows)

Oven-Fried Chicken-on-a-Stick
Calories 204
Fat 6 g
Carbs 16 g
Fiber .7 g
Protein 20 g

In a large bowl, combine the salt, 1 teaspoon of the paprika, ½ teaspoon of the onion powder, and ½ teaspoon of the garlic powder. Add the buttermilk and whisk until the salt is completely dissolved and the spices are dispersed in the liquid.

Cut the chicken lengthwise into about 1-inch-wide strips. Add to the marinade and let stand at room temperature for 30 minutes. (Do not marinate any longer or the chicken will be too salty. If you can't cook it right at the 30-minute mark, remove the chicken from the marinade and refrigerate until ready to continue.)

In a large shallow dish (a 9 by 13-inch baking dish works well), combine the bread crumbs, the remaining 1 teaspoon paprika, the remaining ½ teaspoon of onion powder, and the remaining ½ teaspoon of the garlic powder. Add the 2 tablespoons oil and toss well to coat. Whisk together the egg whites and mustard in a second large shallow dish. Season both mixtures with pepper.

Preheat the oven to 350°F. Line a rimmed baking sheet with aluminum foil, then set an ovenproof rack on it. Coat the rack with nonstick cooking spray.

CONTINUED

Remove the chicken from the marinade, shaking off any excess, and thread onto sixteen 12-inch bamboo skewers, dividing the meat evenly, about 1 strip per skewer. Dip the chicken into the egg mixture, coating both sides. Place in the bread crumb mixture one skewer at a time, sprinkle with crumbs to cover, and press so the coating adheres to both sides. Gently shake off any excess crumbs and place the skewers on the prepared rack.

Bake the chicken, turning halfway through, until golden brown and the juices run clear, about 25 minutes. Serve warm with the dipping sauce.

VIDALIA–HONEY MUSTARD DIPPING SAUCE
MAKES 2¼ CUPS

Put the vinegar, onion, garlic, honey, and mustard in the bowl of a food processor fitted with the metal blade. Pulse until smooth. With the motor running, add the oil in a slow steady stream until thick and emulsified. Taste and adjust for seasoning with salt and pepper. Store in an airtight container for up to 3 days.

¹/₄ cup apple cider vinegar

1 Vidalia onion, peeled and quartered

1 garlic clove

¹/₃ cup honey

2 tablespoons Dijon mustard

¹/₂ cup canola oil

Coarse kosher salt and freshly ground black pepper

Vidalia–Honey Mustard
Dipping Sauce per tablespoon
Calories 42
Fat 3 g
Carbs 4 g
Fiber .1 g
Protein .1 g

CHICKEN, APPLE, *and* CHEDDAR BURGERS

SERVES 4

At The Varsity drive-in in Atlanta, the staff has a language all its own. They bellow "what'llyahave? what'llyahave?" as you enter. Founded in 1928, the menu includes burgers, hot dogs, as well as hand-cut onion rings and French fries. If you say, "French fries," the counter man calls out "Strings!" to those behind the line. A hamburger with mustard is a "Yankee steak," derisively referring to its yellow streak; onions on the side make it "sideways"; and a "glorified steak" is a hamburger with mayo, lettuce, and tomato.

I'm not sure what the folks at The Varsity would call this sweet, cheesy, juicy concoction—but I know they'd love it. The apple provides both sweetness and moisture, and baking the burgers at high heat means they cook quickly and don't dry out. A generous dollop of whole-grain mustard adds a spicy component, making this low-fat alternative burst with flavor.

1 medium sweet-tart apple (such as Gala, Granny Smith, Cortland, or Fuji), cored and quartered

$1/4$ sweet onion

1 pound ground chicken or turkey

3 garlic cloves, very finely chopped

$1/2$ jalapeño chile, cored, seeded, and finely chopped

2 ounces sharp Cheddar cheese, grated ($1/2$ cup)

2 tablespoons chopped fresh flat-leaf parsley

Coarse kosher salt and freshly ground black pepper

Calories 237
Fat 14 g
Carbs 4 g
Fiber .4 g
Protein 23 g

Preheat the oven to 425°F. Line a rimmed baking sheet with a silicone mat or parchment paper. Grate the apple on the large side of a box grater (if you grate the apple skin-side out, you can grate it without having to peel it—a bit of peel is okay). Then, grate the onion and the cheese. In a medium bowl, combine the chicken, apple, onion, garlic, chile, Cheddar, and parsley. Season with salt and pepper. Divide into 4 equal size balls; each will weigh about 7 ounces. Shape each into a patty about 4 inches in diameter. Place directly on the prepared baking sheet.

Transfer to the oven and roast until lightly browned, flipping once during cooking, and the temperature measures 165°F when measured with an instant-read thermometer, about 18 minutes. Serve immediately.

PATTY TIME!

The best way to make sure raw ground meat is seasoned properly is to take a teaspoon or two and cook it in the microwave or in a small skillet for a few minutes until the mixture is cooked all the way through; then taste and adjust the seasoning with additional salt and pepper.

BASIL-PEACH CHICKEN BREASTS

SERVES 6

Georgia produces over 130 million pounds of peaches a year. Some states may grow more, including South Carolina and California, but Georgia is deservedly known as "The Peach State," the result of the efforts of a farmer in Marshallville, Georgia, who bred the Elberta peach from the seed of a Chinese cling peach in the late 1800s. I am loyal to Georgia peaches. My high school was located in Marshallville, Georgia—in the middle of the state, with school breaks dictated by peach season, and with many of my classmates being the sons and daughters of Georgia farmers. The red clay and the hot sun create a taste unlike no other.

Bright and slightly sweet, peaches and basil are a great flavor combination. The technique of starting the chicken on the stovetop and finishing in the oven helps prevent dry, overcooked chicken. The flavorful jus is fresh and clean, much lighter than a flour-thickened gravy.

3 boneless, skinless chicken breasts (1½ pounds)

Coarse kosher salt and freshly ground black pepper

1 tablespoon pure olive oil

1 shallot, thinly sliced

1 teaspoon grated fresh ginger

2 garlic cloves, very finely chopped

12 basil leaves, finely chopped, plus more whole leaves for garnish

1 cup homemade chicken stock (see note, page 78) or reduced-fat, low-sodium chicken broth

4 large peaches, peeled, pitted, and sliced ¼-inch thick (about 2 cups)

Calories 169
Fat 5 g
Carbs 6 g
Fiber .9 g
Protein 24 g

Preheat the oven to 350°F.

Pat the chicken dry on both sides with paper towels. Season the chicken on both sides with salt and pepper. Heat the oil in a large ovenproof nonstick skillet over medium-high heat until shimmering. Add the chicken and cook until browned, about 2 minutes per side. Remove to a plate and set aside.

Decrease the heat. Add the shallot and cook until translucent, about 3 minutes. Add the ginger and garlic to the pan and cook until fragrant, stirring constantly, 45 to 60 seconds. Add the chopped basil, chicken stock, and peaches. Return the chicken to the pan and turn to coat. Transfer to the oven. Bake until the juices run clear when the chicken is pierced with the point of a knife, about 15 minutes. Serve immediately.

IT'S A-PEELING

Peeling peaches can be tricky business. Often a serrated peeler can be effective, but if the peaches are too ripe, you simply wind up with a handful of puree. To avoid this, bring a small pot of water to a rolling boil. Meanwhile, fill a bowl with ice water. Then, using a paring knife, cut an "X" in the blossom end of the peach. Gently place the peach into the boiling water for 15 to 30 seconds. Remove with a slotted spoon and transfer to the bowl of ice water. The "X" will open slightly and the skin can be removed by gently pulling off with the paring knife.

SLOW-COOKED BARBECUE PULLED CHICKEN

SERVES 8

When I was young, during the hot summer, we spent many days and nights at Clark's Hill Lake on the Georgia–South Carolina border. On Saturdays, friends and family would caravan, coolers and wooden picnic baskets laden with food in tow, out to a campground. I remember learning how to swim with my sweet Mama holding me up in the water, and making mud pies in the shallows with my sister, Jona. We would play hide-and-seek in the piney woods and comb the shores for both real Native American arrowheads and imagined pirate treasures. Lunchtime would come and one of the moms would call the kids up from the man-made sandy beach. We'd plop down with sweaty red faces at the picnic tables to paper plates filled with pulled pork sandwiches, potato salad, and coleslaw.

I use healthier chicken breasts for this variation, which can either be prepared in a medium slow cooker or in the oven. Serve on whole wheat buns with a side of Sassy Slaw (page 50) to help create your own summer memories.

1 (14.5-ounce) can no-salt-added diced tomatoes

¼ cup apple cider vinegar

2 tablespoons honey

1 tablespoon smoked paprika

1 tablespoon soy sauce

1 tablespoon Dijon mustard

¼ teaspoon red pepper flakes

4 boneless, skinless chicken breasts (2 pounds)

Coarse kosher salt and freshly ground black pepper

Sweet and Tangy Barbecue Sauce (page 29), for accompaniment

Calories 167
Fat 3 g
Carbs 9 g
Fiber .7 g
Protein 25 g

Slow cooker method: Combine the tomatoes, vinegar, honey, paprika, soy sauce, mustard, and red pepper flakes in the insert of a medium slow cooker. Add the chicken and season with salt and pepper. Cover with the lid and cook on low until the chicken is falling apart, about 5 hours. Taste and adjust for seasoning with salt and pepper.

Oven method: Preheat the oven to 350°F. Combine the tomatoes, vinegar, honey, paprika, soy sauce, mustard, and red pepper flakes in a medium Dutch oven. Add the chicken and season with salt and pepper. Bring to a boil over high heat. Cover with the lid and transfer to the oven. Cook until the chicken is falling apart, 1½ to 2 hours. Taste and adjust for seasoning with salt and pepper. Serve warm.

SPICY CREOLE TURKEY CUTLETS
WITH HOLY TRINITY TOMATO GRAVY

SERVES 6

This recipe is loosely based on grillades (pronounced "gree-ahds"), traditionally a cutlet of veal, pork, or beef simmered in Creole gravy. Food lore suggests the original dish may have originated when butchers sliced thin pieces of fresh pork and pan-fried it with sliced onions. The grillades were then eaten over grits or rice throughout the day as a working man's lunch. In N'awlins, they enjoy this rib-sticking feast for breakfast and brunch. However, it is certainly substantial enough to serve as supper.

In classic French cooking, a mirepoix is the vegetable base made of onion, carrot, and celery used for soups, stocks, and sauces. The term "holy trinity" of Cajun cooking irreverently plays off the Catholic heritage in Louisiana, and is slightly different than the French mirepoix as it is a trio of onion, celery, and green bell pepper. (Here I'm using poblano chile because I think green bell pepper comes back to say "hello" too often.) Jazz things up with the New Soul Creole Dirty Rice (page 86) for a soulful, satisfying combination of meat and gravy.

1¹/₂ pounds turkey cutlets

1 tablespoon Homemade Creole Seasoning (recipe follows)

1 tablespoon canola oil

1 sweet onion, chopped

1 stalk celery, diced

1 poblano chile, cored, seeded, and diced

2 garlic cloves, very finely chopped

1 tablespoon unbleached all-purpose flour

1 (14.5-ounce) can no-salt-added diced tomatoes

2 bay leaves, preferably fresh

Coarse kosher salt and freshly ground black pepper

Hot sauce

2 green onions, trimmed and chopped, for garnish

Season the cutlets on one side with Creole seasoning. Heat the oil in a large nonstick skillet over medium-high heat. Working in batches, sear the turkey cutlets on both sides, about 2 minutes per side. Remove to a plate.

Decrease the heat to medium. Add the onion, celery, and chile and cook until the onion is soft and translucent, 3 to 5 minutes. Add the garlic and cook until fragrant, 45 to 60 seconds. Add the flour and stir to combine. Add the tomatoes and bay leaves. Season with salt and pepper.

Return the turkey cutlets to the skillet with any juices that may have accumulated on the plate. Nestle the cutlets into the gravy and spoon some of the gravy over the turkey. Shake over a couple of drops of hot sauce. Cover and cook until the turkey is firm and the juices run clear when pierced with a knife, 5 to 7 minutes. Taste and adjust for seasoning with salt and pepper. Top with chopped green onions and serve immediately.

Calories 189
Fat 3 g
Carbs 10 g
Fiber 2 g
Protein 29 g

HOMEMADE CREOLE SEASONING

MAKES ABOUT 1 CUP

1/3 cup cayenne pepper

1/4 cup coarse kosher salt

1/4 cup freshly ground white pepper

3 tablespoons dried thyme

1 tablespoon freshly ground
black pepper

2 teaspoons dried sage

1 teaspoon onion powder

1 teaspoon garlic powder

Many of the store-bought Creole seasonings are mostly salt, sometimes with added preservatives and anticaking agents. Anticaking agent sounds like a government spy who has a serious problem with baked goods. This simple seasoning blend is a mixture of salt, pepper, and dried herbs and spices.

In a small airtight container or mason jar, combine the cayenne, salt, white pepper, thyme, black pepper, sage, onion powder, and garlic powder. Stir to combine. Store in a cool, dry place for up to 3 months.

POWDER POWER

I most often use fresh spices for the best flavor, but there are times when powdered spices are powerful flavor enhancers. Powdered spices are also less likely to burn over high heat, and when doubled-up with fresh spices, they allow for a double-dose of satisfying flavor.

TURKEY MEATLOAF
WITH MUSHROOM GRAVY

SERVES 8

Meatloaf is an all-American classic. I'll be the first to admit that when you substitute healthier ground turkey for the ground beef, you lose a bit of savory punch. But adding mushrooms to the mix adds flavor and texture without adding fat. Cremini mushrooms are simply baby portobello mushrooms. They are dark-brown and slightly firmer than white button mushrooms. They also have a slightly fuller flavor than their paler relations. Look for mushrooms with no bruises, closed gills, and a rounded cap that ranges from $1/2$ to 2 inches in diameter. If you cannot find cremini, plain white button mushrooms will work.

MEATLOAF

1 teaspoon canola oil, plus more for pan

1 sweet onion, finely chopped

1 carrot, grated

12 ounces cremini mushrooms, stems trimmed and chopped

Coarse kosher salt and freshly ground black pepper

2 garlic cloves, chopped

2 teaspoons low-sodium Worcestershire sauce

$1/2$ cup chopped fresh flat-leaf parsley

$1/4$ cup low-sodium ketchup

1 cup fresh whole wheat bread crumbs (from about 2 slices of whole wheat bread)

1 large egg, lightly beaten

1 large egg white

$1^1/_4$ pounds ground turkey

Mushroom Gravy, for accompaniment (recipe follows)

Preheat the oven to 400°F. Spray a large casserole with nonstick cooking spray. Set aside.

Heat the oil in a large sauté pan over medium heat. Add the onion and cook until clear and translucent, about 3 minutes. Add the carrot and cook, stirring, until softened, about 1 minute. Add the mushrooms, season with salt and pepper, and cook, stirring occasionally, until the liquid from the mushrooms has evaporated, 8 to 10 minutes. Add the garlic and cook until fragrant, 45 to 60 seconds. Remove from the heat; add Worcestershire sauce, parsley, and ketchup. Transfer the vegetables to a large bowl to cool slightly. Add the bread crumbs, turkey, egg, and egg white. Season with salt and pepper and mix well with your hands. (So that you can taste and adjust for seasoning, simply zap a teaspoon or so in a bowl in the microwave. Add salt and pepper as needed.)

Scoop the mixture into the prepared casserole and shape into a loaf about 9 inches long and 4 to 5 inches wide. Transfer to the oven and bake until an instant-read thermometer inserted into center registers 165°F, 45 to 50 minutes. Remove to a rack to cool and tent loosely with foil. Let the meatloaf stand 5 minutes before serving with mushroom gravy.

CONTINUED

1 tablespoon pure olive oil

2 tablespoons unbleached
all-purpose flour

1 pound mixed mushrooms (such
as cremini, chanterelle, morel,
shiitake, and white button), sliced

Coarse kosher salt and freshly
ground black pepper

2 cups homemade chicken stock
(see note, page 78) or reduced-fat,
low-sodium chicken broth

Calories 247
Fat 12 g
Carbs 17 g
Fiber 3 g
Protein 20 g

MUSHROOM GRAVY

MAKES 2 CUPS

Heat the oil in a large skillet over medium heat. Add the flour and
stir to combine. Add the mushrooms and season with salt and pepper. Cook until tender, about 5 minutes. Whisking constantly, add
the stock mixture to the roux. Bring to a boil over medium-high
heat, stirring constantly, and cook until the sauce thickens, about
5 minutes. Taste and adjust for seasoning with salt and pepper.

LEAN ON ME

Make sure you check the label on ground turkey or chicken. For the
leanest option you want all breast meat. If it doesn't specify breast
meat, it might contain skin or dark meat, which have added fat. Trust
me, you don't need the fat: you can add moisture in other ways, as
I've done here with the mushrooms in Turkey Meatloaf with Mushroom Gravy (page 137) or the apple in the Chicken, Apple, and Cheddar Burgers (page 129).

SWEET TEA-BRINED TURKEY TENDERLOIN
WITH CHILE-PEACH GLAZE

SERVES 6

Make sure to look closely at the package when you are buying the tenderloins. Some of the packaged turkey tenderloins that are labeled "natural" have up to 30 percent added "flavor solution," which basically means you are paying for water and salt. I vastly prefer to create my own flavor solution (that is, brine). Brining lean meats like turkey is a simple and easy technique, since it helps the turkey absorb additional liquid during cooking. The meat loses some of its liquid while cooking, but since the meat is juicier to begin with, it cooks up juicier at the end.

1/4 cup coarse kosher salt

1/4 cup firmly packed dark brown sugar

2 cups boiling water

2 family-size tea bags

3 cups ice cubes

1 1/2 pounds turkey tenderloin

2 peaches, pitted and coarsely chopped (about 2 cups)

1/2 red chile, such as bird's eye or Thai, cored, seeded, and coarsely chopped

2 tablespoons honey

1 slice fresh ginger, (about the size of a quarter), chopped

Coarse kosher salt or freshly ground black pepper

1 teaspoon canola oil

Calories 151
Fat 2 g
Carbs 8 g
Fiber .8 g
Protein 29 g

Combine the salt and brown sugar in a heatproof bowl. Add the boiling water and stir to dissolve, then add the tea bags and steep for 5 to 7 minutes. Add the ice cubes and stir to cool. Add the tenderloin, cover the bowl with plastic wrap, and refrigerate to marinate, about 30 minutes. Remove from the brine, rinse well, and pat thoroughly dry with paper towels. (Do not brine any longer or the turkey will be too salty. If you can't cook it right at the 30-minute mark, remove the turkey from the marinade and refrigerate until ready to continue.)

Preheat the oven to 350°F. Meanwhile, place the peaches, chile, honey, and ginger in the jar of a blender or bowl of a food processor fitted with the metal blade. Season with salt and pepper. Blend or pulse until a smooth sauce. Set aside.

Heat the oil in a large ovenproof skillet over medium-high heat until shimmering. Add the turkey tenderloin and cook until seared and golden brown on both sides, 2 to 3 minutes per side. Spoon the reserved peach sauce over the turkey. Transfer to the oven and cook until the juices run clear when pierced with a knife and the temperature reads 165°F when measured with an instant-read thermometer, about 25 minutes. Remove to a cutting board and cover with aluminum foil to rest and let the juices redistribute, about 5 minutes. Slice on the diagonal and serve immediately.

ROAST TURKEY BREAST
WITH QUICK ORANGE-CRANBERRY RELISH

SERVES 6

Like many people, for years I only ate roast turkey during the holidays, or on the occasional sandwich. It wasn't until I really started on my weight-shedding journey that I realized how important turkey could be as part of a meal plan. One four-ounce serving of turkey provides 65 percent of your recommended daily amount of protein—and less than 12 percent of the recommended daily allowance of saturated fat. It's a good habit to roast a turkey breast early on Sunday or Monday and then use it for sandwiches and salads for the rest of the work week. Most deli meat, even the all-natural deli meat, contains a great deal of sodium, not to mention stabilizers and such. It's far cheaper and healthier to cook a breast at home.

A half breast on the bone will yield about 1½ pounds of meat, which will serve six people for a dinner-size portion or make about twelve properly portioned sandwiches. When serving, make sure to discard the skin, but save the bones for stock.

TURKEY

2 stalks celery, cut into 2-inch lengths

1 sweet onion, sliced

¼ cup white wine

2 garlic cloves, mashed into a paste with salt (see note, page 113)

3 sprigs fresh thyme, leaves only, chopped

5 fresh sage leaves, chopped

1 (2½-pound) turkey breast, on the bone, with skin

Quick Orange-Cranberry Relish, for serving (recipe follows)

Roast Turkey Breast
Calories 120
Fat 3 g
Carbs .6 g
Fiber .18 g
Protein 35 g

Preheat the oven to 350°F.

Place the celery, onion, and wine in the bottom of a medium ovenproof casserole. Combine the garlic, thyme, and sage. Loosen the skin from the meat gently with your fingers and smear the garlic-herb paste directly on the meat. Place the turkey breast on the bed of vegetables. Transfer to the oven and cook until the temperature measures 155°F when measured with an instant-read thermometer, about 1 hour.

Transfer the meat to a cutting board, preferably with a moat, and tent with aluminum foil. Let the meat rest and the juices redistribute for 15 minutes.

To serve, slice into ½-inch-thick slices and place on a warmed serving plate. Drizzle over some of the flavorful broth and serve with a dollop of orange-cranberry relish.

QUICK ORANGE-CRANBERRY RELISH

MAKES 3 CUPS

Finely grated zest of 1 orange

1 orange, peeled, seeded, and coarsely chopped

1 jalapeño chile, cored, seeded, and chopped

$^1/_3$ cup sugar

1 (12-ounce) bag fresh or frozen cranberries (3 cups)

$^1/_4$ cup walnut halves

Coarse kosher salt and freshly ground black pepper

Quick Orange-Cranberry Relish
per tablespoon
Calories 14
Fat .3 g
Carbs 3 g
Fiber .4 g
Protein .1 g

Place the zest, orange, and the jalapeño in the bowl of a food processor fitted with the metal blade and pulse until finely chopped. Add the sugar and cranberries and continue to pulse until berries are coarsely chopped. Add the walnuts and pulse to combine. Season with salt and pepper. Allow the relish to chill for at least 30 minutes, and up to 2 days. Serve relish chilled or at room temperature.

HONEY MUSTARD CAROLINA QUAIL
WITH GRILLED GRAPES

MAKES 8 TO SERVE 4 AS A MAIN COURSE OR 8 AS AN APPETIZER

The men in my family are hunters, and we have always had tidy little bundles of tender quail in the freezer. The trouble is, the men are good hunters—but not always so great at removing the buckshot. The dull sound of metal hitting the plate is not an uncommon sound at our table in the fall. Now, there's no need to risk a tooth. Thanks to places like Manchester Farms, a family-owned business in Columbia, South Carolina, quail are now farmed and widely available in better markets and grocery stores across the country—without pesky pellets as well as in boneless and semiboneless forms.

Cooked quail can be, and should be, pink even when the meat has reached a safe internal temperature—so don't be startled when you cut in and see rosy flesh. This is caused by the unique protein makeup of the meat.

1 tablespoon pure olive oil, plus more for the grill grate

$1/4$ cup dry white wine

2 tablespoons Dijon mustard

1 tablespoon honey

Dash of Worcestershire sauce

8 semiboneless quail (2 pounds)

8 ounces red grapes on the stem, divided into 8 smaller bunches

2 tablespoons chopped fresh flat-leaf parsley

Coarse kosher salt and freshly ground black pepper

Per 2 Quail
Calories 340
Fat 10 g
Carbs 23 g
Fiber 1 g
Protein 38 g

In a large, shallow bowl, combine the 1 tablespoon oil, wine, mustard, honey, and Worcestershire. Add the quail. Cover and marinate at least 4 hours or overnight.

Prepare a charcoal fire using about 6 pounds of charcoal and burn until the coals are completely covered with a thin coating of light gray ash, 20 to 30 minutes. Spread the coals evenly over the grill bottom, position the grill rack above the coals, and heat until medium-hot (when you can hold your hand 5 inches above the grill surface for no longer than 3 or 4 seconds). Or, for a gas grill, turn on all burners to high, close the lid, and heat until very hot, 10 to 15 minutes.

Remove the quail from the marinade and bring to room temperature. Rub the hot grate with a rag dipped in oil. Season the quail with salt and pepper and grill until the meat is firm and the temperature measures 160°F (according to USDA guidelines) when read with an instant-read thermometer, about 4 minutes per side. In the last minute or so of cooking, add the grapes directly on the grill and cook just until lightly charred and slightly wilted, about 1 minute. Remove the quail from the grill and place on a warmed serving platter. Sprinkle with parsley and garnish with the grilled grapes. Serve immediately.

SPATCHCOCK

If your butcher only carries whole quail, you can still prepare this recipe. Simply spatchcock the birds. Spatchcocking allows for quicker cooking and is especially helpful for even cooking when grilling. Place the bird on a clean cutting board, breast side down. Using poultry shears, make a lengthwise cut on both sides of the backbone from neck to tail. Remove the backbone and save it for stock. Open the bird like a book. Proceed with the recipe. For larger birds such as Cornish game hens and chickens, place the bird on a baking sheet, breast side up, top with a second baking sheet, and weight it down in the refrigerator with a brick or several large cans of tomatoes for several hours or overnight. The meat cooks quicker and more evenly.

CHAPTER 7

PORK, BEEF, *and* LAMB

YOU WERE PROBABLY WONDERING if I was going to include this chapter at all—after all, pork, beef, and lamb, generally speaking, aren't the lightest or healthiest foods in the world. But the truth is, sometimes you know you just want a bone to gnaw on, something savory and meaty that brings out your inner caveman. If the preceding chapters have proved one thing, it's that vegetables and salads can be awfully satisfying. But that doesn't mean that pork, beef, and lamb have to be cut from your healthy eating plan entirely. You simply must make smart choices about the cut and the cooking method. And, of course, pay attention and eat a practical portion—the best and most surefire way to lighten up.

The pig has always been an important staple food in the South. It's been said that if cotton was king, then pig was queen. Swine provided the South with a stable supply of meat; pigs reproduce more frequently than cattle and sheep. Pigs were also easier to care for, and corn, perhaps the princess of Southern agriculture royalty, was used to feed and fatten the animals. Pork in some form

or another often seasons traditionally prepared vegetables, appears on most Southern tables as a roast or chops, and is found slow-smoking in pits all across the South. Pigs were first introduced in the 1500s to what is now the southeastern United States by Spanish explorer Hernando de Soto. In fact, the famous hogs of Ossabaw Island, off the coast of Georgia, are descendants of those pigs brought to the New World by de Soto. Over time, some of the Spanish pigs escaped and became feral in southeastern forests.

But nowadays, few people are eating these heritage breeds of pork, and most of what's sold in supermarkets is conventionally raised pork, primarily the breed American Yorkshire. These pigs are grown on large farms, sometimes called CAFOs. Defined by the Environmental Protection Agency, CAFO means Concentrated Animal Feeding Operation. It's large-scale farming. This pork has been bred and fed to be leaner than their heritage-breed counterparts—some pork tenderloin is as lean as skinless chicken breast, and loin roasts and loin chops are also relatively low in fat.

That said, I really think you should give the heritage breeds you might find at your local farmers' market a try. Berkshire, Mangalitsa, and Red Wattle pigs are often not as lean, but their meat is intensely flavored and supremely satisfying. Many of these breeds are raised on small farms and don't have the negative environmental impact of factory farming; moreover, the care and stewardship is often more humane, as are the methods of slaughter.

All pork must be sufficiently cooked to eliminate disease-causing parasites and bacteria. However, today's pork can be safely enjoyed when cooked to an internal temperature of 145°F. The meat will be pale pink, moist, and tender. Bourbon Grilled Pork Chops with Peach Barbecue Sauce is great for weekend grilling and Pulled Pork Tenderloin with Red Pepper Vinegar Sauce is simple and quick, great for a weeknight supper. Cider-Braised Pork Loin with Apple-Thyme Jus is deceptively easy and great for dinner parties and Sunday suppers. The leftovers make a mean sandwich, too!

Beef and lamb were a bit slower to the Southern table, but have become a part of the modern American diet. Leaner cuts of beef include eye of round roast or steak, sirloin tip side steak, top round roast and steak, bottom round roast and steak, and top sirloin steak. You don't necessarily have to sacrifice flavor by choosing lean cuts of beef. My recipes are intense with flavors such as vinegar, coffee, cocoa, and mustard.

I've made a lot of changes in my diet these past few years and one of them is eating less beef. But, sometimes . . . I crave a rich, juicy steak.

So, now, when I eat beef, I want it to be good, really good. I want it to be good for me and I want it to be good for the planet. Granted, I can't do it all the time, but for the most part, I try to buy and eat grass-fed beef.

Dispensing antibiotics to healthy animals has become rote on the large cattle farms that dominate American agriculture. Medical experts increasingly condemn the practice and say it contributes to the emergence of antibiotic-resistant bacteria.

Grain-fed cattle spend most of their lives eating grass in pastures, and then move on to a feedlot where they eat an inexpensive, high-calorie grain diet for three to six months. Grain-fed beef raised in this manner is the most widely produced type of beef in the United States.

Grass-fed beef is beef that is raised solely on grass, not raised on grass then finished on corn. Grass-fed beef is leaner and can be more challenging to cook because it doesn't have as much forgiving fat, but grass-fed beef is most often very full-flavored and exceptionally meaty.

Regardless of your choice of grain-fed or grass-fed, this chapter will help you dress up your table with Rack of Lamb with Pecan-Mint Dipping Sauce, snuggle in for some down-home comfort with Coffee-Braised Pot Roast, and celebrate the holidays with Spinach and Parmesan–Stuffed Beef Tenderloin.

CIDER-BRAISED PORK LOIN
WITH APPLE-THYME JUS

SERVES 8

Riverview Farms is a certified organic family farm on two hundred acres in the beautiful Appalachian foothills of northwest Georgia. In the fertile bottomlands of the Coosawattee River, two generations of the Swancy family (Carter and Beverly Swancy purchased the farm in 1975; their three grown sons—including Wes and his wife, Charlotte—now work the farm as well) grow certified organic vegetables, Berkshire pork, and grass-fed beef.

According to the USDA, the average American agrarian is a white male aged fifty-five or older. Charlotte is a young dynamo! She's a mom and a marketer, an accountant and an activist. I have immense respect for her; she's one of the hardest working women that I know. Charlotte and Wes are the faces of the new American farmer. If you have access to farm-raised meats, like Riverview Farms, make sure to support your local farmer.

1 tablespoon pure olive oil

1 (2-pound) center-cut boneless pork loin

1 sweet onion, sliced

2 cups apple cider

$1/4$ cup apple cider vinegar

4 apples, such as Granny Smith or Honeycrisp, cored and quartered, plus more for garnish

3 thyme sprigs, plus more for garnish

2 bay leaves, preferably fresh

2 garlic cloves, very thinly sliced

Coarse kosher salt and freshly ground black pepper

Calories 298
Fat 12 g
Carbs 22 g
Fiber 2 g
Protein 26 g

Preheat the oven to 350°F.

Heat the oil over high heat in a large skillet until shimmering. Add the meat and brown on all sides, about 8 minutes. Remove to a plate. Decrease the heat to medium. Add the onion and cook, stirring occasionally, until golden brown, about 5 minutes. Add the cider and apple cider vinegar and stir to combine. Return the pork and any juices that have collected on the plate to the skillet. Surround it with the four quartered apples and toss in the sprigs of thyme and bay leaves.

Transfer to the heated oven. Cook, turning and basting occasionally, until the pork is tender and an instant-read thermometer inserted into the center of the meat registers 140°F to 145°F, 35 to 45 minutes, depending on the shape of thickness of the loin. The pork will be slightly pink in the center (this is desirable).

Transfer the pork to a cutting board, preferably with a moat. Tent with aluminum foil to keep warm. Let it rest for about 10 minutes. Meanwhile, taste the cider jus and adjust for seasoning with salt and pepper. Slice the pork loin into slices about $1/4$ inch thick and place on a warmed serving platter. Pour over some of the apple-thyme jus and top with the apples.

Garnish with additional thyme leaves and serve the remaining jus on the side.

BOURBON GRILLED PORK CHOPS
WITH PEACH BARBECUE SAUCE

SERVES 4 AND MAKES 3 CUPS SAUCE

Pork chops are a tender, quick-cooking cut of meat. In fact, so quick-cooking, that they are actually very easy to overcook. Cooking these chops on the bone, instead of using boneless chops, will help the pork cook more evenly, and make them less likely to dry out. Just make sure to trim away as much fat as possible for healthier results. The tangy Peach Barbecue Sauce, flavored with the zip of ginger and vinegar, and sweetened with natural honey, would be incredible on grilled or roasted chicken, as well.

I'll be honest with you, this is a splurge meal since we're cooking the meat on the bone and serving it with barbecue sauce—a plan-for-it, make-sure-to-work-out-that-day dinner. But, it's worth it! I find it so depressing for someone to say to me, "Oh, you can't have that on your diet, can you?" It's not about "no," it's about saying "yes!" I can have anything as long as I am accountable with my exercise and stick to my plan. So, believe me, I am going to gnaw on this bone until it shines.

4 peaches (about 1¼ pounds), halved, pitted, and quartered

2 medium ripe tomatoes, seeded and quartered

1 tablespoon canola oil

1 sweet onion, chopped

1 tablespoon finely chopped fresh ginger

¼ cup apple cider vinegar

¼ cup honey

2 tablespoons bourbon

¼ cup coarse kosher salt, plus more for seasoning

Freshly ground black pepper

¼ cup firmly packed brown sugar

2 cups boiling water

3 cups ice cubes

4 center cut, bone-in pork chops, about 1-inch thick, well trimmed, (2¾ to 3 pounds)

In the bowl of a food processor fitted with the metal blade, puree the peaches and tomatoes until smooth; set aside. Heat the oil in a medium saucepan over medium-high heat until shimmering. Add the onion and cook, stirring occasionally, until golden brown, 5 to 7 minutes. Add the ginger and cook, stirring frequently, until fragrant, 1 to 2 minutes. Add the reserved peach-tomato puree, vinegar, honey, and bourbon; season with salt and pepper. Bring the mixture to a boil over high heat, then decrease the heat to simmer. Cook until the mixture is reduced by half and thickened, about 20 minutes. Taste and adjust for the seasoning with salt and pepper. Reserve ¼ cup sauce for basting the chops, and keep the remaining sauce warm in the saucepan until ready to serve.

Meanwhile, place the remaining ¼ cup salt and brown sugar in a medium heatproof bowl. Pour over the 2 cups boiling water and stir to dissolve. Add the ice cubes and stir to cool. Add the pork chops, cover the bowl with plastic wrap, and refrigerate to marinate, about 30 minutes. (Do not marinate any longer or the pork will be too salty. If you can't cook it right at the 30-minute mark, remove the pork from

CONTINUED

Pork Chop
Calories 327
Fat 13 g
Carbs 7 g
Fiber .4 g
Protein 44 g

Peach Barbecue Sauce
per tablespoon
Calories 19.18
Fat .4 g
Carbs 4 g
Fiber .4 g
Protein .3 g

the marinade and refrigerate until ready to continue.) Remove from the brine, rinse well, and thoroughly dry pat with paper towels. Set aside.

Season the pork chops with pepper. Prepare a charcoal fire using about 6 pounds of charcoal and burn until the coals are completely covered with a thin coating of light gray ash, 20 to 30 minutes. Spread the coals evenly over the grill bottom, position the grill rack above the coals, and heat until medium-hot (when you can hold your hand 5 inches above the grill surface for no longer than 3 or 4 seconds). Or, for a gas grill, turn all burners to high, close the lid, and heat until very hot, 10 to 15 minutes.

Or, preheat a grill pan over medium-high heat until hot. Place the pork chops in the grill pan or on the grill and grill for 3 to 5 minutes per side or until the internal temperature reaches 145°F, brushing with Peach Barbecue Sauce in the last few minutes. Remove to a plate and cover with aluminum foil to rest and let the juices redistribute, 3 to 5 minutes. Serve immediately with reserved warm sauce on the side.

GRILL FRIEND

An instant-read thermometer is your best friend when it comes to cooking meat on the grill. Sometimes it's hard to gauge the doneness of the meat, especially when you've got hot and cold spots on the grill, distractions like kids running around the yard, and the inevitable conversation magnet that a grill can be. An accurate digital instant-read thermometer will be your best grill-friend who will save you from overcooked chops or underdone chicken.

PULLED PORK TENDERLOIN
WITH RED PEPPER VINEGAR SAUCE

MAKES 4 CUPS TO SERVE 8

Pulled pork is traditionally a slow-cooked shoulder, shredded by hand into tender, succulent threads of meat, then doused with sauce. (My slow cooker chicken version pays a nod to this version, too; see page 132.) This variation uses a much leaner and quicker cooking cut of meat—the tenderloin. It's a far cry from low- and slow-cooked shoulder, but the good news is that comes in far lower in saturated fat and is perfect for a splendid weeknight supper.

RED PEPPER VINEGAR SAUCE

1 (14.5-ounce) can no-salt-added tomato puree

$1/_2$ cup apple cider vinegar

$1/_2$ cup apple juice

1 tablespoon dark brown sugar

1 teaspoon red pepper flakes

Coarse kosher salt and freshly ground black pepper

PORK TENDERLOIN

1 tablespoon canola oil

$1^1/_2$ pounds pork tenderloin

Coarse kosher salt and freshly ground black pepper

Red Pepper Vinegar Sauce
per tablespoon
Calories 8
Fat .1 g
Carbs 2 g
Fiber .2 g
Protein .2 g

Pulled Pork Tenderloin
Calories 144
Fat 4 g
Carbs 10 g
Fiber 1 g
Protein 17 g

To make the sauce, combine the tomato puree, vinegar, apple juice, sugar, and red pepper flakes in a small stainless steel saucepan and bring to a boil over high heat. Season with salt and pepper.

To make the pork, preheat the oven to 350°F. Line a rimmed baking sheet with heavy-duty aluminum foil. Heat the oil in a large skillet over medium-high heat until shimmering. Season the pork with salt and pepper, then sear the tenderloin until well browned on all sides, 5 to 7 minutes.

Remove from the heat and place the tenderloin lengthwise on the prepared baking sheet. Top with about 1 cup of the red pepper vinegar sauce and roll to fully coat. Fold the foil over the top of the meat and pinch the ends of the foil to seal well. Bake until very tender, 30 to 45 minutes.

Remove from the oven and transfer the pork to a cutting board. Tip the cooking juices into a large bowl. Using a chef's knife, chop the pork and add to the bowl with the cooking juices. Add sauce to taste, about $1^1/_2$ cups. Taste and adjust for seasoning with salt and pepper. Serve with the remaining sauce on the side.

COCOA-CRUSTED TOP SIRLOIN
WITH MUSHROOMS

SERVES 4

The USDA advises that a 1-pound steak should serve four people. Even I'll admit that when I see three or four slices of steak on my plate, I get a bit depressed. When I want a steak, I really want a meaty, juicy *steak*. So, I am suggesting a compromise. Cook the steak and weigh out the recommended portion, instead of just plopping a ¹⁄₂ pound—or more—of steak on your plate, and top it with the amazing, mushroomy sauce. The rich, earthy cocoa powder melts into the rich beef with superb, hearty results, and the mushrooms turn this into a veritable umami bomb. If you really want to go back for more, you can make that choice—or have scrumptious leftovers the next day, but I think you'll be pleased with this ultra-meaty meal!

RUB

2 tablespoons cocoa powder

1 tablespoon firmly packed dark brown sugar

2 teaspoons coarse kosher salt

¹⁄₄ teaspoon ground cinnamon

¹⁄₄ teaspoon ground ginger

¹⁄₄ teaspoon freshly ground black pepper

Pinch cayenne pepper

1 (1-pound) top sirloin steak, about 1¹⁄₂ inches thick

2 teaspoons pure olive oil

8 ounces mushrooms (such as cremini, chanterelle, morel, shiitake, and white button), sliced

2 tablespoons chopped fresh flat-leaf parsley

Coarse kosher salt and freshly ground black pepper

Calories 157
Fat 7 g
Carbs 4 g
Fiber .7 g
Protein 20 g

To make the rub, in a small bowl, combine the cocoa powder, sugar, salt, cinnamon, ginger, black pepper, and cayenne. Stir to combine.

Adjust the oven rack to the middle position and preheat oven to 350°F. Place an ovenproof rack over a rimmed baking sheet. Set aside.

Pat the steak dry with paper towels and season on one side with the cocoa-spice rub.

Heat the oil in a large skillet over medium-high heat just until smoking. Place the steak, rub-side down, in the skillet and cook for 15 seconds to sear the spice crust. (Don't cook it any longer or the brown sugar will burn.) Flip to sear the other side, about 3 minutes. Transfer to the prepared rack and roast the steak until medium-rare and an instant-read thermometer inserted into the center of the meat registers 125°F, about 15 minutes.

Meanwhile, once you have transferred the steak, immediately add the mushrooms to the skillet and season with salt and pepper. Cook, stirring occasionally, until golden brown. Add the parsley and toss to combine. Taste and adjust for seasoning with salt and pepper.

Transfer the steak to a warmed serving platter, tent with aluminum foil, and let rest for 10 minutes. (Yes, 10 minutes. That way all the juices remain in the steak and don't run out onto the cutting board. And, you'll be topping it with hot mushrooms, so it's going to be just fine.) Remove any fat on the edges and cut into ½-inch slices.

Serve topped with mushrooms.

HELPFUL HINT

Nobody wants to feel hungry or unsatisfied when trying to lose weight. One method of making sure you feel satiated and aren't tempted to overindulge is to eat what's really good for you first. Start with the vegetables or salad, for example. It's especially helpful when you are working on portion control. You will fill up with fiber, and, if you listen to your body, you will be more likely to be satisfied with a smaller amount of protein than you are used to. I find this eating technique to be especially helpful at dinnertime.

SPINACH *and* PARMESAN-STUFFED BEEF TENDERLOIN

SERVES 15

Beef tenderloin is the most expensive cut of meat. It's the gold standard of beef because, not surprisingly given its name, it's the most tender. In beef, exercise means flavor, so the leg muscles are intensely flavored, but very tough. These cuts are more appropriate for long, slow cooking, like pot roast. The muscles along the back of the cow don't get much exercise; these are the quick-cooking steaks like rib eye and New York strip that come from the primal cut called the loin. Underneath the loin is the tenderloin, which gets even less exercise than the loin.

The truth is that the tenderloin actually doesn't have a lot of flavor. That's why you most often see it wrapped in bacon or served with a horseradish cream sauce. In this stunning dish appropriate for a holiday feast, I've stuffed it with a savory combination of spinach and Parmesan, which really bumps up the flavor.

1 (3^1/$_2$-pound) beef tenderloin, trimmed

Coarse kosher salt and freshly ground black pepper

6 garlic cloves, very finely chopped or mashed into a paste with salt (see note, page 113)

1 cup cooked spinach (thawed if frozen), squeezed dry and chopped

^{1}/$_2$ cup freshly grated Parmigiano-Reggiano cheese

2 tablespoons pure olive oil

Calories 291
Fat 22 g
Carbs .9 g
Fiber .3 g
Protein 20 g

Preheat the oven to 425°F.

Using a sharp knife, butterfly the tenderloin by cutting it open lengthwise, taking care not to cut all the way through and leaving a spine so you can open the tenderloin like a book. (Or ask your butcher to do it.) Season generously inside and out with salt and pepper. Rub the garlic paste on the inside of the tenderloin. Spread the spinach over the inside surface to cover. Sprinkle with the Parmesan cheese.

Reform the tenderloin and tie every 3 inches with kitchen twine to hold in the filling. Heat the oil in a large roasting pan and sear the meat on all sides over high heat. Roast until an instant-read thermometer inserted in the center of the meat and stuffing reads 120° to 125°F for medium-rare meat (the internal temperature of the meat will continue to rise about 10°F outside of the oven), about 20 to 25 minutes.

Remove to a carving board, preferably with a moat, and tent to keep warm. If serving hot, let stand for 10 to 15 minutes before carving. If serving at a buffet, cool for at least 30 minutes, then carve and serve within 2 hours. Or cool completely, wrap tightly in aluminum foil, and refrigerate for up to 2 days before carving and serving at room temperature.

RACK OF LAMB
WITH PECAN-MINT DIPPING SAUCE

SERVES 4

Mama has never been a big fan of lamb, but I have grown to love it. I find a rack of lamb to be a perfect celebration supper. The faintly sweet meat pairs nicely with the tangy yogurt sauce. Make sure the butcher removes the chine bone, also known the backbone, and that he cracks the rack between the ribs so you can easily cut it into chops.

LAMB

1 rack of lamb (about 1 1/2 pounds)

Coarse kosher salt and freshly ground black pepper

2 tablespoons Dijon mustard

2 garlic cloves, very finely chopped

1/4 teaspoon red pepper flakes, or to taste

1 teaspoon pure olive oil

PECAN-MINT DIPPING SAUCE

1 cup plain 2 percent Greek yogurt

2 garlic cloves, chopped

2 tablespoons chopped pecans

2 tablespoons chopped fresh mint, plus whole sprigs for garnish

2 tablespoons chopped fresh cilantro, plus whole sprigs for garnish

Coarse kosher salt and freshly ground black pepper

Rack of Lamb
Calories 309
Fat 22 g
Carbs 2 g
Fiber .1 g
Protein 23 g

Pecan-Mint Dipping Sauce
per tablespoon
Calories 16
Fat .9 g
Carbs .8 g
Fiber .1 g
Protein 1 g

Preheat the oven to 375°F.

To make the lamb, remove the meat from the refrigerator 15 minutes before roasting. Season the rack with salt and pepper. In a small bowl, combine the mustard, garlic, and red pepper flakes to form a paste.

Heat the olive oil in a heavy-duty ovenproof skillet over high heat. When the oil is very hot, brown the lamb, 3 to 5 minutes per side. Flip the rack so the meat is right side up. Brush the mustard paste all across the top of the rack to coat. Immediately place the hot pan in the oven. Roast until an instant-read thermometer inserted in the thickest part reads 135°F, 12 to 15 minutes. Turn the oven to broil and cook for a few minutes until the mustard coating is golden brown, about 2 minutes, depending on the strength of your broiler.

Meanwhile, to make the sauce, in a small bowl, combine the yogurt, garlic, pecans, mint, and cilantro. Season with salt and pepper.

Remove the skillet and transfer the rack of lamb to a carving board, preferably with a moat. Cover with aluminum foil and let rest about 5 minutes before slicing to let the juices redistribute. Slice between the bones, forming either single or double chops.

Place on a warmed serving platter and garnish with additional mint or cilantro. Serve immediately with the dipping sauce on the side.

GRILLED BALSAMIC FLANK STEAK

SERVES 6

"Against the grain" is a phrase used when cutting meat. It makes sense—unless you have no idea what it means. Meat is made of long muscle fibers aligned parallel to one other in bundles. The term *grain* refers to the direction. Some muscles, like the tenderloin, are finely grained and you can't really tell which way they are aligned. However, muscles such as flank steak have thicker muscle bundles and a coarser grain. Cut with the grain, the result is muscle fibers that are long, stringy and tough. Cut against the grain, and you cut short muscle fibers that are short and tender. Serve this flavorful steak warm with vegetables, or tossed with a salad the next day.

$1/4$ cup balsamic vinegar

2 tablespoons Dijon mustard

1 tablespoon pure olive oil

$1/2$ teaspoon onion powder

$1/2$ teaspoon garlic powder

1 ($1^1/_2$-pound) beef flank steak

Coarse kosher salt and freshly ground black pepper

Calories 166
Fat 7 g
Carbs .7 g
Fiber 0 g
Protein 22 g

Combine the vinegar, mustard, oil, and onion and garlic powders in a large sealable bag or container and stir to combine. Add the steak. Turn a few times to coat the steak. Cover or seal and marinate, in the refrigerator, turning occasionally, for at least 30 minutes and up to 2 hours. Remove from the marinade and season with salt and pepper.

Prepare a charcoal fire using about 6 pounds of charcoal and burn until the coals are completely covered with a thin coating of light gray ash, 20 to 30 minutes. Spread the coals evenly over the grill bottom, position the grill rack above the coals, and heat until medium-hot (when you can hold your hand 5 inches above the grill surface for no longer than 3 or 4 seconds). Or, for a gas grill, turn on all burners to high, close the lid, and heat until very hot, 10 to 15 minutes.

Grill the steaks to your desired doneness, about 4 minutes per side for medium-rare. Remove to a clean plate and set aside for 2 to 3 minutes to rest and let the juices redistribute.

Slice the steaks against the grain into $1/4$-inch strips and serve immediately.

RAISING THE STEAKS

Marinades are made up of three components: acid, oil, and herbs or spices. The acid helps to partially denature the meat's proteins, opening up channels in the meat where flavor can seep in, but marinades mostly penetrate only the surface. If you want the flavor of the marinade to completely coat the meat, I suggest that you reserve some of the marinade (before adding the raw steak) to toss with the cut, cooked meat.

COFFEE-BRAISED POT ROAST

SERVES 8

Eye of round is from the rear leg of the steer and is a lean and fairly tough cut of meat. It needs low and slow cooking to coax the meat into tenderness. The addition of the anchovies is optional, but will give the meat a mighty umami boost, a handy technique to enhance the characteristic taste of the beef, while reducing the amount of fat. A "cup of Joe" may seem like a very odd addition to pot roast, but the full and slightly acidic taste of the coffee is a robust addition to the gravy.

1 (3-pound) eye of round

Coarse kosher salt and freshly ground black pepper

1 tablespoon pure olive oil

2 sweet onions, chopped

1 carrot, chopped

1 stalk celery, chopped

2 garlic cloves, chopped

4 anchovies, chopped (optional)

2 cups homemade chicken stock (see note, page 78) or reduced-fat, low-sodium chicken broth, plus more if needed

1 cup freshly brewed coffee

Bouquet garni (see note, page 166)

Calories 282
Fat 9 g
Carbs 8 g
Fiber 1 g
Protein 40 g

Remove the meat from the refrigerator and season all over with coarse kosher salt. Let rest at room temperature for at least 1 hour. Adjust the oven rack to the lower-middle position and preheat the oven to 350°F.

Season the meat all over with pepper. Heat the oil in large, heavy-duty Dutch oven over medium-high heat. Add the meat and sear until dark brown on all sides, about 5 to 7 minutes. Remove to a plate. To the drippings in the pan, add the onions, carrot, and celery. Season with salt and pepper. Cook, stirring occasionally, until the vegetables start to brown, about 5 minutes. Add the garlic and cook until fragrant, 45 to 60 seconds. Add the anchovies, stock, coffee, and bouquet garni. Return the seared roast to the pot. Cover and transfer to the oven. Roast until the meat is tender, about 3 hours.

Remove and discard the bouquet garni. Transfer the roast to a cutting board, preferably with a moat, and tent with aluminum foil to keep warm. In the Dutch oven, using an immersion blender, puree the sauce and vegetables until smooth. Or, once the beef is removed, ladle the sauce and vegetables into a blender and puree until smooth, a little at a time. Cook the pureed sauce over medium-high heat until the sauce coats the back of a spoon; if needed, thin with more stock to achieve this consistency. (I find that the vegetables are too overcooked to serve alongside the roast, but pureeing them with the gravy adds body and flavor.) Taste and adjust for seasoning with salt and pepper.

Slice the roast against the grain into ½-inch-thick slices. Transfer the meat to a large serving platter. Ladle some of the sauce over the meat and serve the remaining sauce on the side. Serve immediately.

CHAPTER 8

SOUPS

and

STEWS

THERE'S A MYTHICAL CONCOCTION that exists only on the Internet: it's called "Magic Soup," and it can help you lose seven pounds in a week! It keeps company with similarly illustrious and illusory potions such as the Master Cleanse (a detox drink comprised solely of warm water, cayenne pepper, and lemon juice), the Grapefruit Diet (pounds melt away as a result of the powerful fat-melting enzymes in citrus fruit!), and the like. Well, first of all, if you eat nothing but grapefruit and drink nothing but warm water, of course you are going to lose weight. It's not a very sustainable method of losing weight, and I have to wonder how long those pounds stay off, but yes, you will lose weight. I'm certain none of these methods are appropriate for me. I am certain I would mortally wound someone if all I could eat was spicy, warm, lemon water or grapefruit, and I'd be sent to prison in short order. I don't like stripes and orange is not my color.

Soup, however, can help you lose weight! No, it's not magic. Soup feels more filling per calorie because of the liquid content. Research has proven that soup will help us feel full longer compared with eating the same foods without liquid. Think about a cup of carrots, for example. Now think about a cup of carrots in a cup of broth. It's much more filling, takes up more room in the stomach, which in turn quells the appetite more quickly than a salad would. There are actually hormones at work here: specifically ghrelin, which is released in the stomach and is thought to signal hunger to the brain. (Ghrelin just sounds like an evil troll-like gremlin, doesn't it?) Soup can aid in quelling ghrelin because you will feel fuller. That's real!

The hearty aroma of a bubbling soup or sumptuous stew is destined to whet appetites and bring folks into the kitchen. Soup makes memories. Steamy kitchen windows and tantalizing aromas in the air often mean a slowly cooked winter stew is simmering and gently burbling away in the kitchen. When it's cold and wet outside, very few meals satisfy and satiate our souls and stomachs like a steaming bowl of hearty goodness. There's also something very rewarding about making a pot of soup. Perhaps it's because soup is greater than the sum of its parts. There are countless simple and quick soup recipes. And, if you keep onions, carrots, celery, and stock in your kitchen, you can have a bowl of nourishing soup in a flash by using up leftover vegetables or meat from the night before.

Need a pick-me-up? Try a cup of soothing broth instead of a handful of salty snacks. You can say "yes" to comfort food in a bowl of soup. How about Creamy Broccoli-Parmesan, Chicken Tortilla, and Chunky Chicken Noodle? Don't forget Garlic Chicken and Greens with Cornmeal-Herb

Dumplings! Fall wouldn't be the same without a piping hot bowl of spicy chili. There are soups for summer, too, like briskly refreshing Peach and Tomato Gazpacho and rich Georgia Shrimp and Corn Chowder.

Soup is a great way to eat a little less without feeling like you are depriving yourself. Starting a meal with a cup of soup helps you feel more full and more contented. Let's get cooking and stir the pot!

CREAMY BROCCOLI-PARMESAN SOUP

MAKES 8 CUPS TO SERVE 6

This is a creamy, homemade soup made with real, recognizable ingredients (as opposed to all those unpronounceable chemicals that appear on the side of the store-bought soup can). It's true, cheese can be high in fat—but it's also packed with protein, calcium, and vitamins A and D. Plus, if you use cheeses that are full of complex, strong flavors, like Parmigiano-Reggiano, you'll find that a little goes a long way.

In this recipe, I use the entire head of broccoli—stems, too. You're paying for those stems, so you may as well use them! Plus, it bumps up the nutritional content even more. I ask you to really pack the broccoli in the pot, so depending on the size of your saucepan, you may need to add a bit more stock to completely submerge the vegetables. Try it with half broccoli, half broccoli raab—a leafier, slightly spicier cousin of broccoli that also goes by the name of rapini—for a soup that has a little extra zip.

2 cups 2 percent milk (more if needed), warmed

2 cups homemade chicken stock (see note, page 78) or reduced-fat, low-sodium chicken broth, warmed, plus more if needed

1 tablespoon canola oil

1 sweet onion, chopped

1 stalk celery, chopped

2 tablespoons unbleached all-purpose flour

2 pounds of broccoli, cut into florets, with stalks peeled and chopped

Coarse kosher salt and freshly ground black pepper

2 cups packed baby spinach

1/2 cup freshly grated Parmigiano-Reggiano (2 ounces)

1/2 teaspoon cayenne pepper

Calories 167
Fat 7 g
Carbs 18 g
Fiber 4 g
Protein 11 g

Combine the milk and the stock in a small saucepan or in a large liquid measuring cup and warm over low heat or in the microwave. Keep warm.

Heat the oil in a medium saucepan over medium heat until shimmering. Add the onion and celery and cook, stirring occasionally, until the onion is soft and translucent, 3 to 5 minutes. Add the flour and stir to combine. (The mixture will be very dry.) Add the reserved warm milk–stock combination and whisk to combine. Bring to a boil over medium-high heat.

Add the broccoli stalks and season with salt and pepper. Bring to a boil over medium-high heat then decrease the heat to simmer. Cook, uncovered and stirring occasionally, until the broccoli stems tender, about 10 minutes. Add the florets and stir to combine. Continue to cook until tender, about 8 minutes. Add the spinach and stir to combine and wilt the spinach.

To finish the soup, in the stockpot, using an immersion blender, puree the soup. (It will take a few minutes with the immersion blender.) Or, ladle the soup into a blender and puree until smooth a little at a time. Leave it coarse and chunky if you prefer a more rustic soup or puree until smooth for a more elegant soup. Add the cheese and cayenne; stir to combine. Taste and adjust for seasoning with salt and pepper. If needed, rewarm the soup over medium-low heat. Ladle into warmed serving bowls and serve immediately.

CHICKEN TORTILLA SOUP

MAKES 9 CUPS TO SERVE 6

One of the greatest compliments I ever received in the kitchen was from a native Texan with Mexican ancestry who commented that this soup tasted like her grandmother's version. Now, my friends, that is some mighty high praise.

Southern cuisine is alive and changing and is reflected in recipes like this one. There are now huge populations of Latin Americans in the South and their presence has certainly spiced up Southern food. There are also large Asian and Indian communities, mostly in the larger cities, but their effects are penetrating into the smaller towns and countryside, as well. Southern food has changed and is affected by these global influences. The food of South is now equally catfish and churrasco, barbecue and bulgogi, teacakes and tortilla soup.

The technique of charring the tomatoes creates a wonderfully smoky soup. This soup can be made ahead up to the point of adding the green onions, fresh cilantro, and lime juice. Serve along with a side salad for a full meal. It's a more substantial meal with the chicken, but is also great as a full-flavored broth for sipping.

3 (6-inch diameter) corn tortillas

1 tablespoon pure olive oil

Coarse kosher salt and freshly ground black pepper

2 tomatoes, cored

1 sweet onion, chopped

2 garlic cloves, peeled

6 cups homemade chicken stock (see note, page 78) or reduced-fat, low-sodium chicken broth

1 bay leaf, preferably fresh

$1/4$ teaspoon ground cumin

$1/4$ teaspoon ground coriander

$1/4$ teaspoon cayenne pepper

Preheat the oven to 400°F. Line a baking sheet with a silicone baking mat.

Brush one side of each tortilla with a bit of oil; cut the tortillas in half. Stack the halves and cut crosswise into $1/4$-inch-wide strips. Spread the strips on the prepared baking sheet. Season with salt and pepper. Bake until light golden, about 10 minutes. Cool on the baking sheet. Set aside.

Heat a medium skillet over high heat. Add the cored tomatoes and cook, in the dry skillet, until both tomatoes are charred on all sides, about 5 minutes. Transfer to the bowl of a food processor fitted with the metal blade.

In the same skillet, heat the remaining oil over medium heat. Add the onion and cook until translucent, 3 to 5 minutes. (The onion will also loosen some of the charred bits of tomato from the bottom of the skillet.) Add the garlic and cook until fragrant, 45 to 60 seconds. Add to the bowl of the food processor with the tomatoes. Puree until smooth.

3 boneless, skinless chicken breasts, cut into 1/2-inch cubes (1 1/2 pounds)

4 green onions, trimmed and thinly sliced

1/4 cup chopped fresh cilantro, plus whole leaves for garnish

Juice of 2 limes

2 avocados, peeled, pitted, and chopped, for garnish

Calories 343
Fat 15 g
Carbs 22 g
Fiber 7 g
Protein 32 g

Heat a medium pot over medium-high heat. Add the tomato-onion mixture and cook, stirring occasionally, until thick, about 5 minutes.

Add the chicken stock and stir to combine. Add the bay leaf, cumin, coriander, and cayenne pepper; bring to a boil. Decrease the heat to simmer and cook, partially covered, until the flavors are well combined, 15 to 20 minutes.

Add the chicken; simmer until just cooked through, 5 to 7 minutes. Stir in the green onions, 1/4 cup cilantro, and lime juice. Taste and adjust for seasoning with salt and pepper.

Just before serving, divide the tortilla strips among 6 bowls. Ladle on the hot soup and garnish with avocado and whole cilantro leaves. Serve immediately.

CHUNKY CHICKEN NOODLE SOUP

MAKES 9 CUPS TO SERVE 6

Shhh. Don't tell. This soup is really vegetable soup with just enough chicken and noodles in it to warrant the name. And I've got another secret: it starts with a rotisserie chicken. Because, guess what? If you start with a store-bought rotisserie chicken and work in a little zip, you can have homemade soup on the table in just about 30 minutes. You'll have a bit of chicken left over for sandwiches and salads, too.

Cooking is not only about making good food; it's also about working smart and not wasting. Make sure to save the bones from the chicken. If you save the bones from the chicken, celery ends, carrot peelings, mushroom trimmings, and onion skins, you are well on your way to making stock. It's a freebie. And, if you don't feel like doing it now, just pop it all in a freezer bag and do it later.

2 teaspoons pure olive oil

1 sweet onion, chopped

1 carrot, chopped

1 celery stalk, chopped

1 garlic clove, very finely chopped

8 ounces sliced cremini mushrooms

Coarse kosher salt and freshly ground black pepper

12 cups homemade chicken stock (see note, page 78) or reduced-fat, low-sodium chicken broth

Bouquet garni (see note, below)

1 medium sweet potato, peeled and cut into 1-inch cubes (about 2 cups)

6 ounces green beans, stem ends trimmed and cut into 1-inch pieces (about 1 1/3 cups)

2 ounces (1 cup) uncooked egg noodles

3 cups shredded rotisserie chicken (about 12 ounces), from 1 (4- to 5-pound) rotisserie chicken

Calories 216
Fat 3 g
Carbs 22 g
Fiber 3 g
Protein 27 g

Heat the olive oil in a large pot over medium heat. Add the onion, carrot, and celery and cook until the onion is soft and translucent, 3 to 5 minutes. Add the garlic and cook until fragrant, 45 to 60 seconds. Add the mushrooms and season with salt and pepper. Cook, stirring occasionally, until the mushrooms start to wilt and brown, about 5 minutes. Add the chicken stock and stir to combine. Add the bouquet garni and sweet potato. Bring to a boil over high heat. Decrease the heat to simmer and cook until the sweet potato is just tender, 15 to 17 minutes.

Add the green beans, egg noodles, and chicken. Stir to combine and poke with your spoon to make sure the beans and noodles are submerged. Simmer until the noodles and green beans are tender, 8 to 10 minutes. Taste and adjust for seasoning with salt and pepper. Ladle into warmed bowls and serve immediately.

THE BOUQUET GARNI

Bouquet garni is a French term to describe a sachet of herbs and seasonings. To make one, simply tie 3 sprigs flat-leaf parsley; 3 sprigs thyme; 1 bay leaf, preferably fresh; and 10 whole black peppercorns together in a cheesecloth.

GARLIC CHICKEN *and* GREENS
WITH CORNMEAL-HERB DUMPLINGS

Why is it that so many Southern classics start with a chicken in a pot? Chicken and dumplings is quite possibly the best cold weather comfort food combination—thick, hearty stew married with fluffy, tender dumplings. Dumplings are essentially biscuits simmered in chicken broth. There are two basic schools of thought when it comes to dumplings: drop, like these, or rolled, in which the dough is rolled out and cut into strips and slipped into the broth. The broth flavors the dumplings and the flour from the dumplings helps to thicken the stew. These dumplings are made with flour combined with whole-grain cornmeal, which boosts their nutritional profile.

Dumplings can be a bit tricky. It's easy to wind up with heavy, paste-like dough balls. Ugh. There are recipes out there using canned biscuits, but with this easy, breezy dump-and-stir drop dumpling, you can have homemade down-home comfort in a snap—made with all-natural, wholesome ingredients.

2 teaspoons pure olive oil

1 sweet onion, chopped

2 stalks celery, chopped

2 carrots, coarsely chopped

6 garlic cloves, finely chopped

2 quarts homemade chicken stock (see note, page 78) or reduced-fat, low-sodium chicken broth

1 bay leaf, preferably fresh

1/2 teaspoon red pepper flakes

1/2 pound collard greens, stemmed and chopped, or 8 cups chopped collards from a bag

3/4 cup unbleached all-purpose flour or whole wheat pastry flour

1/2 cup fine whole-grain cornmeal (not self-rising)

Heat the oil in a heavy-duty pot over medium heat. Add the onion, celery, and carrot and cook until the onion is soft and translucent, 3 to 5 minutes. Add the garlic and cook until fragrant, 45 to 60 seconds. Add the chicken stock, bay leaf, and red pepper flakes; bring to a boil over high heat. Add the collards; decrease the heat to simmer and cook until bright green, about 10 minutes; keep at a simmer.

To prepare the dumplings, in a bowl, combine the flour, cornmeal, cheese, baking soda, thyme, and 1/2 teaspoon of the salt. Add the buttermilk and melted butter to the dry ingredients and stir to combine until the dough forms.

2 tablespoons freshly grated Parmigiano-Reggiano cheese

¹/₄ teaspoon baking soda

1 teaspoon chopped fresh thyme

Coarse kosher salt and freshly ground black pepper

³/₄ cup low-fat buttermilk

2 tablespoons unsalted butter, melted

4 boneless, skinless chicken breasts, cut into 1-inch cubes (2 pounds)

Calories 313
Fat 8 g
Carbs 27 g
Fiber 3 g
Protein 33 g

Using a small ice cream scoop or tablespoon, drop the dough, 1 tablespoon at a time, into the simmering stock. Cover and simmer until the dumplings are partially cooked and the vegetables are just tender, about 10 minutes. Using a wooden spoon, push aside the dumplings and slide the cubed chicken into the greens and broth. Cover again and continue to cook until the dumplings and chicken are cooked through and the collards are tender, an additional 10 to 15 minutes. Taste and adjust for seasoning with salt and pepper. Ladle into warmed bowls and serve immediately.

QUICK *and* EASY TURKEY CHILI

MAKES 9 CUPS TO SERVE 6

The best eating plans include a lot of high protein, low-fat foods. Protein gives your body energy and helps to build muscle instead of fat. A robust chili like this one is both lean and filling. I'm hefty handed with the chile powder to give it some serious umpff! When you buy chile powder, buy dried chiles that have been dried and made into powder, not a mixture of dried chiles, ground herbs, and spices. All too often those blends contain a great deal of salt. My favorite chile powder is pure New Mexican chile powder made from Hatch peppers. It's available online and in better grocery stores.

Make sure you go easy on any add-ons like cheese or sour cream. Instead, try it with the Baked Onion Blossom (page 32) for a seemingly decadent meal.

1 tablespoon pure olive oil

1 sweet onion, chopped

3 large garlic cloves, chopped

1 (28-ounce) can no-salt-added whole tomatoes

2 (14.5-ounce) cans of low-sodium pinto beans, rinsed and drained

1 pound ground turkey

1 carrot, grated

3 cups low-sodium tomato juice

2 bay leaves, preferably fresh

1/4 cup ground dried red chiles

1 teaspoon ground cumin

1 teaspoon ground coriander

1/2 teaspoon cayenne pepper, or to taste

Coarse kosher salt and freshly ground black pepper

Calories 330
Fat 13 g
Carbs 33 g
Fiber 11 g
Protein 20 g

Heat the oil in a large heavy-bottomed pot over medium heat. Add the onion and cook until soft and translucent, 3 to 5 minutes. Add the garlic and cook until fragrant, 45 to 60 seconds. Add the tomatoes, beans, turkey, and carrot. Using a wooden spoon, break up the turkey, then add the tomato juice. Bring to a boil over high heat. Decrease the heat to simmer and add the bay leaves, ground chiles, cumin, coriander, and cayenne pepper. Season with salt and pepper. Simmer, uncovered, stirring occasionally, until the turkey is tender and the flavors have married, about 30 minutes. Taste and adjust for seasoning with salt and pepper.

Ladle into warmed bowls and serve immediately.

DAMN GOOD DAWG CHILI

MAKES ABOUT 9 CUPS TO SERVE 6

Football is a religion in the South and tailgating is its tasty secular communion. My alma mater is the University of Georgia, and our colors are red and black, like this crowd-pleasing, comforting chili. Our mascot is "UGA," an English bulldog. He, like all other good Georgia fans, is known in local parlance as a "damn good dawg" pronounced just like it's written.

I prefer using dried beans over canned. There's no doubt it takes a little bit more effort and planning. The upside is that you can control the amount of salt and any other ingredient that goes in them, how tender or firm the beans are in the final dish, and they are easier on the pocket book. This chili is pretty high in calories, but I think that it's realistic to want 1½ cups of this damn good chili.

³⁄₄ pound ground chicken or turkey sausage

1 pound lean ground beef

2 sweet onions, chopped

5 garlic cloves, chopped

1 jalapeño chile, cored, seeded, and chopped

3 tablespoons dried ground red chiles

1 tablespoon ground cumin

2 (28-ounce) cans no-salt-added whole tomatoes, with juice and coarsely chopped

1¼ cups homemade chicken stock (see note, page 78) or reduced-fat, low-sodium chicken broth

Coarse kosher salt and freshly ground black pepper

2 tablespoons finely ground cornmeal

½ pound dried black beans, cooked (about 3 cups; see note, page 173) or 2 (14.5-ounce) cans no-salt-added black beans, rinsed and drained

Heat a large heavy duty pot over medium heat. Add the sausage, beef, and onions. Cook, stirring often, breaking up the meat, until the meat is no longer pink, 5 to 7 minutes. Add the garlic and jalapeño and cook until fragrant, 45 to 60 seconds. Add the ground chiles, cumin, tomatoes, and chicken stock. Season with salt and pepper. Bring to a boil over high heat, then decrease the heat to simmer. Cook, stirring occasionally, until slightly thickened, about 30 minutes. Add the cornmeal and black beans and stir to combine. Cook, stirring occasionally, until thickened and the flavors have married, about 15 minutes. Taste and adjust for seasoning with salt and pepper.

Go Dawgs! Sic 'em!

Calories 415
Fat 18 g
Carbs 38 g
Fiber 10 g
Protein 32 g

A BIG POT OF BEANS

Dried beans are a lot cheaper that canned ones. One pound of dried beans measures about $2^3/_4$ cups and, once soaked and cooked, will produce 6 cups of cooked beans. Soaking peas and beans overnight often falls under the category of "well-intended but sadly forgotten." If you forget to plan ahead, you can quick-soak the beans in about an hour: First, wash and sort the beans. Place in a large stockpot and add water to cover, about 3 quarts. Bring to a rolling boil over high heat. Remove from the heat and let soak for 1 hour. Drain, discarding the water and return to the pot with an inch of water to cover. Bring to a boil with teaspoon or so of salt. (There's a lot of debate about salting beans during cooking; I salt my beans near the beginning of cooking and taste and adjust for seasoning at the end.) Decrease the heat to simmer and cook until the beans are tender, 45 to 90 minutes, depending on the age of the beans. Drain well and proceed with the recipe.

BEEF *and* FARRO SOUP

MAKES 9 CUPS TO SERVE 6

Normally, beef and barley soup is made with beef shoulder that needs hours and hours of cooking. Top sirloin steak is quicker cooking, well flavored, tender, and yet still considered lean by USDA guidelines. Instead of barley, I am using farro, a hearty ancient grain that is very similar to barley, but quicker cooking, as well.

Although there's actually not a whole lot of meat in this soup, it's still very hearty and robust. Why? First, there's a double dose of mushrooms that contribute to the intense, beefy flavor and second, the meat is cut into small pieces, so each spoonful contains a meaty bite.

2 teaspoons pure olive oil

1 pound top sirloin, cut into 1-inch cubes

Coarse kosher salt and freshly ground black pepper

3 carrots, peeled and diced

2 stalks celery, diced

1 sweet onion, diced

1 pound cremini mushrooms, sliced

4 garlic cloves, finely chopped

4 cups homemade chicken stock or reduced-fat, low-sodium chicken broth

1 ounce dried porcini mushrooms (optional)

1 turnip, peeled and diced

$1/2$ cup semi-pearled farro (see note, page 92)

1 (14.5-ounce) can no-salt-added diced tomatoes in juice

3 sprigs fresh thyme

1 bay leaf, preferably fresh

Snipped fresh chives, for garnish

Calories 258
Fat 6 g
Carbs 28 g
Fiber 5 g
Protein 24 g

Heat 1 teaspoon of the oil in large heavy-bottomed pot over medium-high heat until shimmering. Season the beef with salt and pepper. Add the beef to the pot without crowding, stirring, until the beef is well-browned on all sides, 3 to 5 minutes. (This may take two batches, depending on the size of your pot.) Transfer the beef to a plate.

Decrease the heat to medium and add the remaining oil, carrots, celery, onion, and fresh mushrooms. Cook, stirring frequently, until the mushrooms have exuded their liquid, 5 to 7 minutes. Add the garlic and cook until fragrant, 45 to 60 seconds.

Add the stock, dried mushrooms, turnip, farro, tomatoes with juice, thyme, and bay leaf. Return the beef and any accumulated juices to the pot and bring to a boil over medium-high heat. Season with salt and pepper. Decrease the heat to medium-low and simmer, uncovered, until the farro is tender, about 20 minutes. Taste and adjust for seasoning with salt and pepper. Remove the bay leaf and thyme sprigs.

Ladle into warmed bowls and garnish with snipped fresh chives. Serve immediately.

THE NAME GAME

The sirloin consists of several muscles, and steaks cut from this area, while flavorful, vary in tenderness. Top sirloin is desirable for its versatility. It's located at the top of the steer's butt, so it is also called sirloin butt steak, London broil, or top sirloin butt, depending on your butcher or part of the country.

PORK, SQUASH, *and* CHICKPEA SOUP
WITH COLLARD GREEN PESTO

MAKES 8 CUPS TO SERVE 6

Butternut squash is a hard winter squash with a flavor similar to sweet potato, yet lower in calories and carbs. Its natural sweetness creates a rich aromatic broth for the pork and the chickpeas. It's often available already peeled and cubed in the grocery store—and while this prepared squash is a bit more expensive than buying it whole, it's a real time-saver. You can also try this soup with rutabaga in place of the butternut squash. Poor rutabaga is often the last one left in the CSA (Community-Supported Agriculture) box and all-too-often passed over at the grocery store. They can be intimidating, oddly large, and coated in wax. Rutabaga is in the cabbage-turnip family. The flavor is quite like a carrot without the sweetness. If you aren't able to make the pesto, simply toss the four ounces of chopped collards into the soup at the end of cooking.

1 (1¼-pound) pork tenderloin, cut into 1-inch cubes

Coarse kosher salt and freshly ground black pepper

2 teaspoons pure olive oil

1 sweet onion, chopped

1 carrot, chopped

1 stalk celery, chopped

4 garlic cloves, finely chopped

2 cups homemade chicken stock (see note, page 78) or reduced-fat, low-sodium chicken broth, plus more if needed

1 pound butternut squash, cut into 1-inch cubes

1 (14.5-ounce) can chickpeas, rinsed and drained

1 teaspoon smoked paprika

Collard Green Pesto, for accompaniment (recipe follows)

Season the pork with salt and pepper. Heat the oil in a large heavy-duty pot over medium-high heat. Sear the pork in batches, without crowding, until browned on all sides, 3 to 5 minutes. Remove to a plate.

Decrease the heat to low. Add the onion, carrot, and celery. Cook, stirring, until the onion is tender, 3 to 5 minutes. (The vegetables will loosen the brown bits from the bottom of the pot, helping create flavor for the broth.) Add the garlic and cook until fragrant, 45 to 60 seconds. Add the stock, butternut squash, chickpeas, and paprika. Return the reserved pork and any accumulated juices on the plate to the pot. Season with salt and pepper and stir to combine.

Increase the heat to high and bring to a boil. Cover and decrease the heat to simmer. Cook, stirring occasionally, until the vegetables are tender and the pork is cooked all the way through, about 20 minutes. Taste and adjust for seasoning with salt and pepper.

Ladle the soup into warmed bowls and top with a dollop of the pesto. Serve immediately.

CONTINUED

Pork, Squash, and Chickpea Soup
Calories 239
Fat 6 g
Carbs 22 g
Fiber 4 g
Protein 24 g

PORK, SQUASH, AND CHICKPEA SOUP,
CONTINUED

4 ounces chopped collard greens
(about 4 cups)

Juice of $1/2$ orange

$1/4$ cup chopped pecans

2 tablespoons Parmigiano-Reggiano
cheese

1 tablespoon extra-virgin olive oil

Coarse kosher salt and freshly
ground black pepper

Collard Green Pesto per tablespoon
Calories 27
Fat 2 g
Carbs 1 g
Fiber .5 g
Protein .8 g

COLLARD GREEN PESTO
MAKES ABOUT 1 CUP

Bring a small pot of water to a boil. Add the collards and cook just
until bright green, about 2 minutes. Drain well. Either by hand for
a more rustic consistency, or in the bowl of a food processor fitted
with the metal blade for a smoother texture, chop the collards. Add
the orange juice, pecans, Parmesan, and oil. Stir or pulse to combine.
Taste and adjust for seasoning with salt and pepper.

CHOPPING FIRM VEGETABLES

Butternut squash, rutabagas, and celery root are hard and dense—
and very difficult to chop. I have found that the safest way to cut
these tough vegetables is to press the chef's knife against the vegetable, gradually applying more pressure and using your other hand,
rock the vegetable back and forth into the knife. In essence, you're
holding the knife still and rolling the vegetables into the knife (not
the other way around).

GEORGIA SHRIMP *and* CORN CHOWDER

MAKES 7 CUPS TO SERVE 6

Shrimp season in Georgia usually starts in late spring or early summer and lasts until about December, making this chowder a great dish for summer or early fall when both corn and shrimp are in season. If you aren't on a dock or at the beach, keep in mind that when buying shrimp, the odor is a good indicator of freshness; good-quality shrimp have a slightly saltwater aroma; deteriorating shrimp smell overly fishy and sometimes a bit like ammonia.

1 pound unshelled large shrimp (21/25 count), peeled and deveined, shells reserved

1 sweet onion, coarsely chopped

1 carrot, coarsely chopped

Scraped kernels from 4 ears fresh sweet corn (about 2 cups), cobs reserved and halved

2 cups water

2 teaspoons pure olive oil

1 poblano chile, cored, seeded, and chopped

3 stalks celery, chopped

1 sweet onion, chopped

2 garlic cloves, chopped

1 large russet potato, cut into 1/2-inch cubes (about 6 ounces)

3 sprigs fresh thyme, leaves only

2 bay leaves, preferably fresh

Coarse kosher salt and freshly ground pepper

2 tablespoons unbleached all-purpose flour

2 cups 2 percent milk

12 grape tomatoes, quartered, or 1 ripe tomato, cored and chopped

1/4 cup chopped fresh flat-leaf parsley

Smoked paprika, for garnish

Put the shrimp shells in a medium pot and add the coarsely chopped onion, carrot, and halved corn cobs. (It's all about building layers of flavor.) Top with 2 cups of water. Bring to a boil over medium-high heat and decrease the heat to simmer. Cook until the broth is slightly colored and smells lightly sweet, about 5 minutes. Strain into a bowl, discarding the solids, and set aside.

Heat the oil in a large pot over medium heat. Stir in the poblano, celery, chopped onion, potato, and reserved corn kernels. Add the thyme, bay leaves, 1/2 teaspoon salt, and a few grinds of pepper and cook, stirring, 5 to 7 minutes. Stir in the flour until incorporated, about 2 minutes. Stir in the shrimp stock and milk, then cover and bring to a boil over medium-high heat. Uncover, decrease the heat to medium-low, and gently simmer until the vegetables are tender, about 15 minutes. Remove from the heat. Discard the thyme sprigs and bay leaves.

To finish the soup, in the stockpot, using an immersion blender, puree the soup. Or, ladle the soup into a blender and puree until smooth, a little at a time. Leave it coarse and chunky if you prefer a more rustic soup or puree until smooth for a more elegant soup. Taste and adjust for seasoning with salt and pepper. If needed, rewarm the soup over medium-low heat. Stir in the reserved shrimp and tomato; cook until the shrimp are opaque, about 2 minutes. Add the parsley and taste and adjust for seasoning with salt and pepper. Divide among warmed bowls and sprinkle with paprika. Serve immediately.

Calories 245
Fat 5 g
Carbs 34 g
Fiber 4 g
Protein 20 g

PEACH *and* TOMATO GAZPACHO
WITH CUCUMBER-HERB YOGURT

MAKES 6 CUPS TO SERVE 6

I told my mama about this soup and her slow response, in a very dubious drawl, was "Peaches and tomatoes?" I'll admit my family can be a bit slow sometimes in accepting my version of "new Southern cooking." Guess what? She loved it and I think you will, too. This soup is indeed summer in a bowl. It's light and refreshing, just the right balance of sweet peaches and slightly acidic tomatoes. Best yet, this elegant soup may be made ahead. Take the time to chill the serving bowls, as well, for an extra special touch.

4 large peaches, peeled, pitted and quartered (about 2 cups)

2 large tomatoes, cored and quartered (about 4 cups)

$1/2$ sweet onion, coarsely chopped

3 tablespoons apple cider vinegar

Coarse kosher salt and freshly ground white pepper

$1/3$ cup plain 2 percent Greek yogurt

$3/4$ cup finely diced peeled English cucumber (about 3 inches)

2 tablespoons chopped fresh marjoram or chives, plus more for garnish

1 garlic clove, very finely chopped

Best-quality extra-virgin olive oil, for garnish (optional)

$1/4$ peach, pitted and thinly sliced, for garnish

Combine the quartered peaches, tomatoes, onion, and vinegar in the bowl of a food processor fitted with the metal blade. Season with salt and pepper. Puree until smooth. Transfer to a sealable container and refrigerate until cold, about 1 hour. (Take the time to chill the serving bowls at this time, as well.)

Place the yogurt in a medium bowl. Add the cucumber, chives, and garlic and stir to combine; season with salt and pepper. Cover and refrigerate until ready for use.

When ready to serve, taste and adjust the soup for seasoning with salt and pepper. (Chilling dulls the seasoning so it may need to be adjusted.) Ladle the chilled gazpacho into the chilled bowls. Spoon about 2 tablespoons of the cucumber-yogurt mixture into the center. Garnish with a peach slice and a sprig of marjoram. Drizzle over a few drops of extra-virgin olive oil.

Serve immediately.

IT'S THE PITS

These are two kinds of peaches: clingstone and freestone. Clingstone have flesh that clings to the pit and are riper earlier in the season. Freestone separates more easily and the pit can be removed by hand.

Peach and Tomato Gazpacho
Calories 66
Fat .7 g
Carbs 14 g
Fiber 3 g
Protein 3 g

Cucumber-Herb Yogurt
Calories 6
Fat .1 g
Carbs .6 g
Fiber .1 g
Protein .6 g

CHAPTER 9

BISCUITS, BREAD, *and* BAKED GOODS

WHEN I LIVED IN NEW YORK, I enjoyed the finest bagels and bialys, yet I dreamed of biscuits. When I lived in France, I had my pick of perfect, flaky and buttery pastries, yet I craved biscuits. Don't get me wrong—there's nothing like lox and cream cheese on a warm and toasty bagel and heads have been lost over access to a good baguette, but biscuits are my touchstone. As an avid biscuit maker, I enjoy many forms of biscuits: flaky; cakelike; big, double-handed biscuits called cat-heads; and petite tea biscuits meant for showers and luncheons. There's no doubt in my mind that nothing says Southern comfort like a biscuit. Well, other than corn bread. Corn bread is yet another glory of Southern cooking and far easier to master than the biscuit. As I began the transformation with my eating habits, and wanted to lighten up, y'all, I knew early on that biscuits and corn bread had to be part of the plan.

If you're trying to lose weight, you might think that biscuits, bread, and baked goods are forbidden (and that by giving them a whole chapter

here, I've lost my mind). But the truth is, weight loss is first and foremost about calories. So, even grain-based foods like breads and biscuits can be part of a healthy lifestyle. Regardless of whether you are counting carbs or pumping up with Paleo, the bottom line is calories are what matter the most. Eat too many calories from *anything*, and you'll gain weight; eat less than you burn and you'll lose weight.

Ultimately, it is pretty much all about calories. That having been said, some calories are packed with nutrients and contribute to your health and happiness, while others are nutritionally void and considered "empty calories." As much as I love it in a tender, fluffy biscuit, white all-purpose flour just doesn't have the fiber, vitamins, and good-for-you-ness of whole-grain flours. Why? A grain of wheat is made up of three distinct parts: the bran, endosperm, and germ. The outer covering of the kernel, the bran, is high in insoluble fiber. Insoluble fiber is good for you and, well, keeps you regular. Insoluble fibers speed up the passage of food through your gut and are mainly found in whole grains and vegetables. (The other primary kind of fiber is soluble fiber. Soluble fiber attracts water and forms a gel, which slows down digestion. This also helps make you feel full.) The middle layer of the kernel, or endosperm, contains proteins and carbohydrates. The germ is the innermost portion of the kernel, and is a source of unsaturated fat, B vitamins, and antioxidants. To make white flour, wheat kernels are milled to remove the bran and germ, leaving only the endosperm. This means you lose a lot of fiber, healthy unsaturated fats, and antioxidants. The bottom line is, whole grains are better for us than refined grains.

On the baking aisle, you will often find all-purpose flour, self-rising flour, bread flour, pastry or cake flour, whole wheat flour, and whole wheat pastry flour. All of these wheat flours contain protein, and when you combine flour with water, the proteins create a strong and elastic sheet called gluten. Gluten gives structure to yeast breads, but is not as desirable for tender biscuits and quick breads like muffins. All-purpose flour contains an average amount of protein and can be used for many different recipes. (To complicate matters, Southern all-purpose flour like White Lily brand is milled from soft red winter wheat that has less gluten-forming protein than most national brands. It's actually more like cake flour.) Self-rising flour is simply all-purpose flour that already contains baking powder and salt. Bread flour is high in protein, and pastry and cake flours are low in protein. In regard to whole wheat flour, some is high and some is low in gluten, which means that some whole wheat flour is good for all-purpose baking and is simply labeled "whole wheat flour." Others, like whole wheat pastry flour, are low in gluten and more appropriate for baking.

Southern all-purpose flour is better for biscuit making, but not good for us because it is refined. Whole wheat flour is good for us, but makes a heavy biscuit or baked good. But whole wheat pastry flour is light, more like all-purpose. Both King Arthur and Bob's Red Mill are national brands that are widely available. So, what I have done to increase the nutrition and fiber is to replace some of refined unbleached all-purpose flour with whole wheat pastry flour. It's a low-protein flour made from whole grains. It is much softer and more finely textured than regular whole wheat flour, and baked goods made with it will have a similar consistency to those made with refined all-purpose white flour.

It's not a magic wand and carbohydrate-rich foods are still high in calories, but you can say "yes" to Multigrain Pecan Waffles and Blueberry-Banana Muffins, Buttermilk Biscuits with Turkey Sausage Gravy, and Cheesy Jalapeño Beer Bread Muffins. You can enjoy whole-grain Vegetable Cornbread and light and crispy Cornmeal Griddle Cakes. You can say "yes" to biscuits, bread, and baked goods, keep your head, and lose in your waistline.

BUTTERMILK BISCUITS
WITH TURKEY SAUSAGE GRAVY

MAKES 20 BISCUITS

Biscuits are the ultimate representation of old-timey Southern cooking. Perhaps only fried chicken surpasses the biscuit as the culinary symbol of the South. Once upon a time in a land far away inhabited by grandmothers with berry-stained hands and flour-dusted checkered aprons, biscuits were considered a quick bread, something that could be on the table with few strokes in a bowl of leavened flour, fat, and milk. Then, modern conveniences brought along biscuit mix, canned biscuits, and frozen biscuits—all processed and manufactured in a lab, not a kitchen.

The best biscuits are made from flour, dairy, and fat. These are not fruit and fiber bars. There's no way around the fact that biscuits are high in calories. However, I have swapped out some of the all-purpose flour with whole wheat pastry flour to increase the nutritional value, used low-fat buttermilk, and best of all, backed off on some of the saturated fat by using a combination of butter and canola oil. Calorie-wise, butter and canola oil are about the same, but most of the fat in canola oil is unsaturated. I've created a better-for-you-biscuit. So, when you choose to enjoy a biscuit, I guarantee you're going to love this one.

1¼ cups White Lily or other Southern all-purpose flour, or cake flour (not self-rising), plus more for rolling out

¾ cup whole wheat pastry flour

1 tablespoon baking powder

¼ teaspoon baking soda

¾ teaspoon fine sea salt

2 tablespoons cold unsalted butter, cut into bits and chilled

¾ to 1 cup low-fat buttermilk

1 tablespoon canola oil

Turkey Sausage Gravy, for serving (optional; recipe follows)

Preheat the oven to 500°F.

In a bowl, combine the all-purpose flour, whole wheat pastry flour, baking powder, baking soda, and salt. Using a pastry cutter or two knives, cut the butter into the flour mixture until it resembles coarse meal. Combine the buttermilk and oil. Pour in the buttermilk mixture, and gently mix until just combined.

Turn the dough out onto a lightly floured surface. Knead lightly, using the heel of your hand to compress and push the dough away from you, and then fold it back over itself. Give the dough a small turn and repeat eight or so times. (It's not yeast bread; you want to just barely activate the gluten, not overwork it.) Using a lightly floured rolling pin, roll the dough out ½ inch thick. Cut out rounds of dough with a 2-inch round cutter dipped in flour; press the cutter straight down

Buttermilk Biscuit
Calories 62
Fat 2 g
Carbs 9 g
Fiber .6 g
Protein 2 g

CONTINUED

without twisting so the biscuits will rise evenly when baked. Press the dough together and reroll. (Your first pass should yield about 12 biscuits.)

Place the biscuits on an ungreased baking sheet about 1 inch apart. Bake until golden brown, 10 to 15 minutes. Transfer to a rack to cool just slightly.

Split and serve hot with Turkey Sausage Gravy.

TURKEY SAUSAGE GRAVY

MAKES 3²/₃ CUPS

1 tablespoon canola oil

1 pound ground turkey sausage

Coarse kosher salt and freshly ground black pepper

1 sweet onion, finely chopped

¹/₄ cup whole wheat pastry flour

2 cups 2 percent milk, warmed

1 teaspoon chopped fresh sage

Heat the oil in a large skillet over medium-high heat. Add the sausage and season with salt and pepper. Using a wooden spoon, break up the meat into small pieces. Pour off any excess rendered fat. Add the onion and cook until clear and translucent, 3 to 5 minutes. Add the flour and stir to combine and coat. Add the milk and season with salt and pepper. Bring to a boil then reduce heat to simmer. Let cook, stirring occasionally, until thick, about 5 minutes. Add the sage, taste, and adjust for seasoning with salt and pepper. Serve immediately.

Turkey Sausage Gravy per tablespoon
Calories 22
Fat 1 g
Carbs 1 g
Fiber .1 g
Protein 2 g

VEGETABLE CORN BREAD

SERVES 8

The suggested vegetables here are just that, a gentle suggestion. Mix it up depending on what's in season and fresh at the market. Make it taste good! This recipe will support about five cups of chopped vegetables. Any more and the batter doesn't hold together very well, and any less, it's not really vegetable corn bread. I like to use variety of chiles and leave the seeds in the rings to give the corn bread some kick, but you could remove them or try chopped zucchini, yellow squash, or eggplant. If you use these more watery vegetables, you should par cook them first to remove some of the moisture (this could be as simple as zapping in the microwave and draining off the excess water).

Make sure to seek out whole-grain, not self-rising cornmeal for the best corn flavor. It is also known as "nondegerminated." How's that for a word?

2 tablespoons canola oil

2 cups yellow whole-grain cornmeal

1 teaspoon fine sea salt

1 teaspoon baking soda

6 fresh okra pods, stem ends trimmed, very thinly sliced (about 1 cup)

1 red onion, chopped

Cut and scraped kernels from 2 ears of fresh corn, cut from the cob (about 1 cup)

1 banana pepper, thinly sliced into rings

1 jalapeño chile, thinly sliced into rings

1 small red chile, such as bird's eye or Thai, thinly sliced into rings

1/2 poblano chile, cored, seeded, and chopped

2 cups low-fat buttermilk

1 large egg, lightly beaten

Calories 208
Fat 6 g
Carbs 33 g
Fiber 6 g
Protein 6 g

Preheat the oven to 450°F.

Place the oil in a large cast-iron skillet or ovenproof baking dish and heat in the oven until the oil is piping hot, about 10 minutes.

Meanwhile, in a bowl, combine the cornmeal, salt, and baking soda. Add the okra, onion, corn, banana pepper, and chiles and toss to coat. Set aside. In a large measuring cup, combine the buttermilk and egg. Add the wet ingredients to the dry and stir to combine.

Remove the heated skillet from the oven and pour the hot oil into the batter. Stir to combine, and then pour the batter back into the hot skillet. Bake until golden brown, about 35 minutes. Remove to a rack to cool slightly. Using a serrated knife, slice into wedges and serve warm.

SOUR POWER

Buttermilk and baking soda involve a bit of food science. The baking soda reacts to the acidity in the buttermilk. If you run out of buttermilk, you can't just swap in regular milk. However, you can transform milk into buttermilk! To make reduced-fat buttermilk, for each 1 cup of regular 2 percent milk add 1 teaspoon of distilled white or apple cider vinegar. Within just a few seconds, it turns into buttermilk and works perfectly.

CHEESY JALAPEÑO BEER BREAD MUFFINS

MAKES 12 MUFFINS

Cheesy beer bread would seem to be decidedly off the table for a slim-down Southern cook-book, but it's not! First of all to consider, of course, is portion control. That's why I've made these into muffins, not into loaf bread. Second, I'm increasing the nutritional value of the dry ingredients by using a combination of all-purpose and whole wheat pastry flours. Lastly, I'm dividing the cheese into a fifty-fifty split of reduced-fat and extra-sharp, which means less fat, but equal flavor. (I've tried it with all reduced-fat, and they are mighty good that way, too.)

If you want a bit more heat, you can add another jalapeño; it's going to completely depend on the chile. These muffins are incredible with a piping hot bowl of my Damn Good Dawg Chili (page 172).

1 jalapeño chile, cored, seeded, and chopped

8 ounces (1³/₄ cup) unbleached all-purpose flour

4 ounces (¹/₂ cup plus ¹/₃ cup) whole wheat pastry flour

1 tablespoon baking powder

1 teaspoon fine sea salt

¹/₂ cup freshly grated 75 percent reduced-fat Cheddar cheese (2 ounces)

¹/₂ cup freshly grated extra-sharp Cheddar cheese (2 ounces)

1 (12-ounce) bottle lager-style light beer (such as Sam Adams Light)

1 tablespoon unsalted butter, melted

Calories 150
Fat 4 g
Carbs 22 g
Fiber 1 g
Protein 6 g

Preheat the oven to 375°F. Spray a 12-cup muffin tin with nonstick cooking spray. Set aside.

Place the jalapeño in a small microwave-safe bowl and cook in the microwave on high until softened, about 20 seconds, depending on the strength of your microwave. Set aside to cool.

Whisk together the unbleached all-purpose flour, whole wheat flour, baking powder, and salt. Stir in the cheeses and jalapeño. Slowly add the beer until just combined.

Scoop the mixture into the prepared muffin tin, filling the cups about half full. Brush the top of each one with the melted butter. (Don't skip this step; this small amount of butter goes a long way!) Transfer to the oven and bake until deep golden brown and the temperature of the bread measures 210°F on an instant-read thermometer, 28 to 30 minutes. Remove to a rack to cool slightly before removing from the pan. Serve warm or at room temperature.

LEMON-CHIA SEED CAKE

MAKES 1 LOAF TO SERVE 16

Many recipes for lemon poppy seed cake contain two sticks of butter and two cups of sugar! Yikes. In lightening this simple tea cake up, I've made it slightly less sweet, to be served at breakfast or brunch. It's not overly rich, yet and packed with tart lemon flavor.

I'm also substituting chia seeds for poppy seeds. Chia is considered a super food because it delivers the maximum amount of nutrients with minimum calories. It has several of the same benefits as the other "super seed," flax, but unlike flax seed, you don't need to grind them to gain the health benefits. Chia seeds are high in protein and fiber and contain beneficial omega-3 fatty acids, calcium, and antioxidants. They also absorb up to twelve times their own weight! As they expand, it will make you feel fuller and curb your appetite. You can find chia seeds online, at Whole Foods Market, in health foods stores, and in the health food section of better grocery stores.

1 cup unbleached all-purpose flour, plus more for the pan

$^1/_2$ cup whole wheat pastry flour

1 tablespoon chia seeds

$1^1/_2$ teaspoons baking powder

$^1/_2$ teaspoon baking soda

$^1/_4$ teaspoon fine sea salt

1 cup 2 percent plain Greek yogurt

$^3/_4$ cup granulated sugar

3 large eggs

Finely grated zest of 2 large lemons

$^1/_3$ cup plus 1 tablespoon freshly squeezed lemon juice

2 teaspoons pure lemon extract

1 teaspoon pure vanilla extract

$^1/_2$ cup canola oil

$^1/_4$ cup confectioners' sugar

Calories 177
Fat 9 g
Carbs 21 g
Fiber .9 g
Protein 4 g

Position a rack in the center of the oven and preheat the oven to 350°F. (If using a dark metal pan, preheat the oven to 325 °F.) Generously coat an $8^1/_2$ by $4^1/_2$ by $2^1/_2$-inch metal loaf pan with nonstick cooking spray and dust with flour; set aside.

Combine the flours, chia seeds, baking powder, baking soda, and salt in a medium bowl. Whisk the yogurt, granulated sugar, eggs, lemon zest, $^1/_3$ cup of the lemon juice, lemon extract, vanilla, and oil in a large bowl until well blended. Add the flour mixture to the yogurt mixture, stirring until just combined. Transfer batter to the prepared pan.

Bake until the loaf is golden brown and a toothpick inserted into the center comes out clean, 45 to 50 minutes. Cool the loaf in the pan on a rack 5 minutes. Run a knife around the edge of the pan to loosen the cake, invert onto the rack, turn upright, and cool completely.

Combine the confectioners' sugar and remaining tablespoon of lemon juice in a small bowl, stirring until smooth. Drizzle the glaze over the cooled cake. Using a serrated knife, slice the cake into $^1/_2$-inch pieces and serve immediately. Store in an airtight container for up to 4 days.

BLUEBERRY-BANANA MUFFINS

MAKES 12

That blueberry muffin you're grabbing at the coffee shop in an attempt to be healthy very likely has around 450 calories, and 15 percent of your recommended daily allowance of saturated fat. That's no good!

Breakfast is one of the most important meals of the day. Skipping it to "save calories" is nothing but a bad idea—breakfast gets your metabolism going, and if you miss it, I promise you'll just end up scarfing down too much food at lunchtime! But, I understand. I don't like to eat first thing in the morning, either. I will often have a banana and a coffee to get going then, after I work out, I have some protein, maybe an egg or some yogurt. Good and good for you, if you're looking for a great grab and go, this is it.

2 cups whole wheat pastry flour

²/₃ cup sugar

¹/₂ teaspoon fine sea salt

¹/₂ teaspoon ground ginger

1 teaspoon baking soda

1 large egg

2 ripe, medium bananas, mashed

¹/₂ cup plain 2 percent Greek yogurt

¹/₄ cup canola oil

¹/₂ cup low-fat buttermilk

1 pint fresh blueberries

Calories 184
Fat 6 g
Carbs 31 g
Fiber 3 g
Protein 4 g

Preheat oven to 325°F. Grease a 12-cup muffin pan generously with nonstick cooking spray, including the top surface.

In a medium bowl, combine the flour, sugar, salt, ginger, and baking soda. In a small bowl, whisk together the egg, bananas, yogurt, oil, and buttermilk. Stir the wet ingredients into the dry ingredients just until moistened. Using a rubber spatula, gently fold in the berries.

Divide the batter evenly among the prepared cups (the batter will come to the top of the cups). Bake until a toothpick inserted near the center comes out clean, about 30 minutes, rotating pan halfway through baking. Cool for 5 minutes before removing from pan to a wire rack. Serve warm. Store in an airtight container for up to 4 days.

CORNMEAL GRIDDLE CAKES

My grandmother loved cornmeal griddle cakes. She'd serve them with buttery cabbage and strips of fried fatback. It was her "pantry meal" because she always had the ingredients on hand.

I'll leave the fatback out of the meal, but with a quick, easy recipe like this, you can have home-cooked bread with no additives or preservatives on the table in less than twenty minutes. I've intentionally made these corn cakes just a bit on the dry side and cooked them in the least amount oil possible so they are tailor-made to soak up the broth from soups and stews. This has two benefits: they are the perfect "dunker," and since they are not deep fried, they can be made ahead and successfully reheated without tasting like reheated fried food. You could also top them with Lightened-Up Pimiento Cheese (page 24) or even Smoky Eggplant Dip (page 20) for an interesting nibble.

1 cup yellow whole-grain cornmeal (not cornmeal mix or self-rising cornmeal)

$^1/_2$ teaspoon coarse kosher salt

$^1/_2$ teaspoon baking soda

$^1/_2$ cup low-fat buttermilk

1 large egg white, lightly beaten

1 tablespoon canola oil, plus more for the skillet

1 green onion, trimmed and very thinly sliced

Per Cake
Calories 65
Fat 2 g
Carbs 10 g
Fiber 1 g
Protein 2 g

In a bowl, combine the cornmeal, salt, and baking soda. Set aside. In a large measuring cup, combine the buttermilk, egg white, and the 1 tablespoon oil. Add the wet ingredients to the dry and stir to combine. Stir in the green onion.

Heat a large nonstick skillet over medium-high heat. Coat the bottom with a thin layer of oil. Using a small ice cream scoop or tablespoon, place up to 6 spoonfuls of batter in the pan. (Or, using a tablespoon measure, place 2 tablespoons batter, one on top of the other, in the pan to make six 1-ounce portions.) Using an offset spatula or battercake turner, pat the batter down slightly until it's about $^1/_2$ inch thick. Cook until golden brown on the bottom, then turn and cook until golden brown on both sides, $1^1/_2$ to 2 minutes per side, regulating the heat so the cakes essentially bake in the pan instead of deep frying in the pan. Remove to a rack to cool slightly. Serve warm or at room temperature.

MULTIGRAIN PECAN WAFFLES

MAKES 4 CUPS OF BATTER TO MAKE SIX 8-INCH ROUND WAFFLES

Waffles for breakfast are a really special treat and are mostly reserved for lazy Saturday mornings. Mama loves hers loaded with Cool Whip, but she hasn't met much that she doesn't like topped with the famous nondairy topping. I don't share the same appreciation and prefer my waffles topped with gently warmed maple syrup and maybe a small pat of butter. These waffles are packed with heart-healthy pecans, oats, and whole-grain cornmeal—a great way to start your weekend.

These freeze well, too. You can easily double the recipe and cook the rest after you've finished with breakfast. Once they've cooked, store the waffles, separated with waxed paper, in a sealable freezer container. If I need a healthy quick breakfast on the run, it's just as simple as popping one in the toaster oven, then topping it with a bit of sunflower butter and a few slices of fruit.

2 cups low-fat buttermilk

1/2 cup old-fashioned rolled oats

2/3 cup whole wheat pastry flour

2/3 cup unbleached all-purpose flour

1/3 cup chopped pecans

1/4 cup whole-grain cornmeal

1 1/2 teaspoons baking powder

1/2 teaspoon baking soda

1/2 teaspoon fine salt

1 teaspoon ground cinnamon

2 large eggs, lightly beaten

1 tablespoon canola oil

2 teaspoons pure vanilla extract

Mix the buttermilk and oats in a medium bowl; set aside for 15 minutes. Meanwhile, whisk together the whole wheat pastry flour, unbleached all-purpose flour, pecans, cornmeal, baking powder, baking soda, salt, and cinnamon in a large bowl.

Stir the eggs, oil, and vanilla into the reserved buttermilk-oat mixture. Mix with a rubber spatula just until moistened.

Coat a waffle iron with nonstick cooking spray and preheat. Spoon in enough batter to cover three-quarters of the surface (about 2/3 cup for an 8-inch round waffle iron). Cook until the waffles are crisp and golden brown, 4 to 5 minutes. Repeat with remaining batter. Serve immediately.

Calories 285
Fat 11 g
Carbs 37 g
Fiber 4 g
Protein 11 g

CHAPTER 10

SWEET INDULGENCES

I'M NOT SURE IF you have noticed, but at some point recently, the sign above the baking aisle listing the different ingredients that could be found there was changed to "cake mixes." That says a whole heck of a lot about modern American culture and eating habits.

Contrary to what every book, TV expert, and diet ad is telling you, desserts and sweet indulgences are not some sort of evil, diet-ruining, demon food! Eating a sweet treat now and then is not going to make your weight skyrocket. Eating *too many* desserts and *too many* processed sweets—that's what does the damage.

We sort of lose our mind with sweet indulgences. Maybe the sugar makes us nuts. But here's a crazy idea: Maybe the reason we eat desserts so irresponsibly is because we've told ourselves we can't have them. Maybe the taboo is the problem, and the reason we can't just have one cookie, we have to have ten cookies.

I've seen fitness magazines that tell you to chew some of weirdly flavored gums like root beer float and mint chocolate chip to sate sweet cravings. It makes me cringe just thinking of it. Television commercials will lead you to believe that a cup of

fat-free yogurt tastes just like New York cheesecake. Well, if you believe that, I'll sell you the Brooklyn Bridge.

Truth is, deprivation does not work. It's much better to have a little and be satisfied than to cut yourself off entirely because you'll end up bingeing later. Now, I'm not advocating the "Marie Antoinette Diet"—no cake for breakfast!—but there's a lot of research that suggests that it's productive to scratch that itch every now and then.

Many people think that a diet means the demise of dessert, but eliminating your favorite foods altogether can actually put a halt to a healthy eating plan. There's a difference between eating something indulgent occasionally and eating everything you want all of the time. Most anyone can follow a restrictive diet for a short period of time, but sooner or later, most people will break down and way overindulge on the foods they've been denying themselves. If you manage it properly, you can have your cake and eat it, too. Think of it as sensible splurging.

Modern life doesn't always lend itself to homemade meals, much less homemade desserts. When I was a little girl, my grandmother always had a cake or pie of some sort under the cake dome. Life's just not that way for most of us— and Lord knows, most of us don't need an endless dome of cake! We say "yes" to sweet indulgences the way we are able to say "yes" to all good food— in moderation, with appropriate-size portions. A slice of pie should be about one and one-half inches across the top, a brownie needs to be about a two-inch square, and a cookie should be about a tablespoon. Don't let those small quantities make you feel anxious. Think instead about how good you feel when you treat yourself to a sweet indulgence at the same time you treat your body in a way that will help you thrive.

Some of the same techniques that I employed in the baked goods chapter are used here. For example, some of the unbleached all-purpose flour has been replaced with whole wheat pastry flour as in Brown Sugar–Strawberry Shortcakes and Chasing the Carrot Cake. Low-fat buttermilk replaces cream in Big Rich Texas Sheet Cake and I've got a big surprise with the Salted Caramel Sauce. I've also punched up flavor and reduced the amount of sugar so that the desserts are just sweet enough, but not too sweet. Applesauce replaces some of the fat in Pineapple Right-Side-Up Cake, yet a judicious amount of butter is used where it needs to be. The chocolate desserts are rich, full, and deceptively lighter in calories, but not in flavor. Claire's Cream Cheese Swirl Brownies and Chocolate "Brookies" don't just taste better for lightened up foods—they just flat out taste good. Lighten up, y'all, and pass the cake.

SPA-AAH FRUIT COBBLER

SERVES 10

This is a variation of a homey dessert both my mother and grandmother have made my entire life. Other fruits may be substituted, but peach has always been my favorite. Baking this in cast iron makes for beautiful presentation, as the golden brown batter swells around the fruit.

When I first started teaching cooking lessons at the health spa Rancho la Puerta in Tecate, Mexico, I needed a healthy dessert to serve, so I reworked my family's original. I was terrified to teach at a health spa: I had a vision of supermodels and lithe athletes gliding effortlessly from the infinity pool to the weight room, then on to yoga and mountain hikes. I thought they would toast to life with potassium broth and I would be so hungry at dinnertime it would make me want to gnaw my arm off. Then a personal trainer told me it was better to be slightly overweight and fit than be underweight and unfit. It was a revelation. Granted, an opinion, not a free pass, but it really made me think. I want to be strong and healthy, not just skinny.

COBBLER

¹/₄ cup (¹/₂ stick) unsalted butter

¹/₄ cup canola oil

1 cup whole wheat pastry flour

1¹/₂ teaspoons baking powder

¹/₂ teaspoon fine salt

³/₄ cup 2 percent milk

¹/₃ cup agave syrup

1 teaspoon pure vanilla extract

4 cups sliced fresh peaches

VANILLA CREAM

¹/₂ cup plain 2 percent Greek yogurt

3 tablespoons confectioners' sugar

¹/₂ teaspoon pure vanilla extract

Fresh mint sprigs, for garnish

Preheat the oven to 350°F.

To make the cobbler, place the butter and oil in a 9 by 13-inch ovenproof serving dish or 10¹/₂-inch cast-iron skillet and transfer to the preheated oven to heat, 5 to 7 minutes.

Meanwhile, combine the flour, baking powder, and salt in a bowl. Add the milk, agave syrup, and vanilla and stir to combine.

Remove the hot dish with the melted butter and oil from the oven. Add the butter-oil mixture to the batter and stir to combine. Pour the batter into the hot pan. Spoon the peaches evenly over the batter. Return the pan to the oven and bake until brown and the batter has risen up and around the fruit, 30 to 35 minutes. Remove the cobbler to a rack to cool slightly.

Meanwhile, make the vanilla cream. Combine the yogurt, confectioners' sugar, and vanilla extract in a small bowl and stir. Set aside.

Serve portions of cobbler immediately with vanilla cream, garnished with fresh mint.

Spa-aah Cobbler
Calories 191
Fat 11 g
Carbs 22 g
Fiber 2 g
Protein 2 g

Vanilla Cream
per tablespoon
Calories 21
Fat .3 g
Carbs 3 g
Fiber 0 g
Protein 1 g

BROWN SUGAR–STRAWBERRY SHORTCAKES

MAKES 8

Besides fresh, ripe, succulent strawberries, the key to a great strawberry shortcake lies in the quality of the cake. Forget those stale anemic hockey puck–shaped cakes sold in the produce department. Southern shortcakes are made with sweet biscuits, so say "yes" to these golden brown clouds! As a delicately tangy alternative to whipped cream, I sandwich the strawberries with a sweet vanilla cream made with Greek yogurt.

Raw, or turbinado, sugar is made from the initial pressing of sugar cane. It's slightly coarse and contains more of the natural molasses. Demerara sugar is similar in that it is light brown in color, but has even larger sugar crystals with a more pronounced molasses aroma and flavor. Both sugars shimmer like a jewel crust on top of these tender shortcakes.

$1^1/_4$ cups unbleached all-purpose flour

$1^1/_4$ cups whole wheat pastry flour

$1/_3$ cup firmly packed light brown sugar

2 teaspoons baking powder

$1/_2$ teaspoon baking soda

$1/_4$ teaspoon fine sea salt

2 tablespoons unsalted butter, cut into bits

3 tablespoons canola oil

1 cup low-fat buttermilk

$1/_2$ teaspoon pure vanilla extract

1 tablespoon water (optional)

2 tablespoons raw, turbinado, or demerara sugar (optional)

4 cups sliced strawberries

Vanilla Cream (page 197)

Calories 283
Fat 9 g
Carbs 44 g
Fiber 4 g
Protein 7 g

Preheat the oven to 425°F. Line a baking sheet with parchment paper or a silicone mat.

In the bowl of a food processor fitted with the metal blade, pulse the flours, brown sugar, baking powder, baking soda, and salt. Add the butter and oil and pulse until the mixture resembles meal. Add the buttermilk and vanilla. Process until the dough pulls together. (It will be very soft.)

Using a rubber spatula, transfer the dough to a floured board. Knead several times so the dough comes together. Pat evenly into an 8-inch circle about $1/_2$-inch thick. Cut out rounds of dough with a $2^3/_4$- or 3-inch round cutter dipped in flour; press the cutter straight down without twisting so the shortcakes will rise evenly when baked.

Place the shortcakes on the prepared baking sheet. Gather the dough together and repeat with remaining dough. Brush the shortcakes with water and sprinkle with raw sugar. Transfer to the oven and bake until golden brown, about 12 minutes. Remove to a rack to cool slightly.

Toss the strawberries with the remaining tablespoon of raw sugar in a medium bowl.

To serve, split the shortcakes horizontally. Spoon the strawberries and juice onto the bottoms, top with the cream mixture, and replace the shortcake tops. Serve immediately.

BAKED APPLE HAND PIES
WITH SALTED CARAMEL SAUCE

MAKES 12 HAND PIES

Hand pies make me smile. My grandmother use to make them in the fall and they are a very special taste memory. They are such an old-school dessert, most often made with biscuit dough and skillet fried to nutty golden brown. Think country Pop-Tart. I've mixed things up in this instance; tender, flaky pastry envelops apples simmered with just enough sugar and warm spices.

I'm particularly excited about this Salted Caramel Sauce and I know you are going to love it. Caramel sauce is typically made from sugar, heavy cream, and butter—not a good candidate for lightening up. Here I'm using low-fat evaporated milk, a shelf-stable canned milk product with about 60 percent of the water removed from fresh milk to mimic the cream and just enough butter to give it a silky texture.

2 cups unsweetened applesauce

1 teaspoon firmly packed dark brown sugar

$1/8$ teaspoon ground cinnamon

$1/8$ teaspoon ground ginger

Pinch of fine sea salt

1 disk Yogurt Piecrust (page 204)

Unbleached all-purpose flour, for rolling out

1 tablespoon raw, turbinado, or demerara sugar, for sprinkling (optional)

Salted Caramel Sauce, for accompaniment (recipe follows)

Baked Apple Hand Pies
Calories 110
Fat 6 g
Carbs 13 g
Fiber 1 g
Protein 2 g

Place the applesauce in a medium nonstick skillet over medium heat. Cook, stirring often, until the applesauce is thick and has reduced to one cup, about 15 minutes. (It's necessary to cook some of the moisture out of the applesauce so the pies aren't soggy.) Add the brown sugar, cinnamon, ginger, and salt and stir to combine. Transfer to a shallow bowl and place in the refrigerator to cool.

Preheat the oven to 425°F. Line a rimmed baking sheet with parchment paper or a silicone mat.

Roll the piecrust disk to $1/8$ inch thick. Cut out rounds of dough with a 3-inch round cutter dipped in flour; press the cutter straight down without twisting so the dough will rise evenly.

For each hand pie, place about a tablespoon of applesauce just to one side on a dough circle. Dip your finger in a bit of water and using your wet finger, dampen the outer edge of the dough. Fold the dough over, using your fingertips to remove any air pockets. Dip the tines of a fork in flour and press to seal. Place on the prepared sheet pan without touching. Brush with water and sprinkle over the turbinado sugar. Transfer to the oven and bake until nutty golden brown, 18 to 20 minutes. Serve warm, drizzled with Salted Caramel Sauce.

CONTINUED

BAKED APPLE HAND PIES WITH
SALTED CARAMEL SAUCE, CONTINUED

1 cup sugar

¹/₄ cup water

¹/₂ cup low-fat evaporated milk

2 tablespoons unsalted butter

1 vanilla bean, split and scraped, or
1 teaspoon pure vanilla extract

Sturdy pinch of fine sea salt

Salted Caramel per tablespoon
Calories 70
Fat 2 g
Carbs 14 g
Fiber 0 g
Protein .6 g

SALTED CARAMEL SAUCE
MAKES 1 CUP

Combine the sugar and water in a small heavy saucepan. Heat over medium-high heat, swirling the pan occasionally, until the sugar dissolves. Continue to cook, without stirring, until it begins to turn golden around the edges, about 7 minutes (it is important not to stir, or the syrup may crystallize).

When the syrup begins to color, remove from the heat, and very gradually add the milk. (Be very careful because the syrup will furiously bubble up in the pan.) Add the butter. Return the pan to low heat and whisk vigorously until the caramel is completely dissolved, about 3 minutes. Add the scraped vanilla bean and a pinch of salt. Stir to combine. Serve warm or at room temperature.

Store the cooled sauce in an airtight container in the refrigerator for up to 1 month; it will solidify. Reheat it over a double boiler or in a heavy saucepan over very low heat.

OLD-FASHIONED BUTTERMILK PIE

MAKES ONE 11-INCH PIE TO SERVE 16

Buttermilk pie is old-fashioned, country cooking. Once upon a time, buttermilk was the liquid left behind after churning butter out of cream. It was naturally low in fat because most of the fat became the butter. Now, most buttermilk is made from adding cultures to low-fat milk. Many people assume because of its name and thickness that it's high in fat, but that's not true, at all. If you're scared to try it, just remember it's creamy and tangy just like yogurt.

$^3/_4$ cup sugar

3 tablespoons unbleached all-purpose flour

Pinch fine sea salt

1 cup low-fat buttermilk

3 large eggs

$^1/_4$ cup ($^1/_2$ stick) unsalted butter, melted

1 teaspoon pure vanilla extract

$^1/_4$ teaspoon freshly grated nutmeg

1 partially blind-baked Yogurt Piecrust (page 204)

Calories 155
Fat 8 g
Carbs 17 g
Fiber .5 g
Protein 3 g

Preheat the oven to 350°F.

Whisk the sugar, flour, and salt together in a medium bowl or quart measuring cup with a spout. Once combined, whisk in the buttermilk, eggs, and butter. Whisk until the butter is completely incorporated. Add the vanilla and nutmeg. Pour into the blind-baked crust and cover the edge of the crust with strips of aluminum foil. Return to the oven and bake until set, about 45 minutes. Remove to a rack to cool.

Let cool completely before slicing.

YOGURT PIECRUST

MAKES TWO 22-OUNCE DISKS

The crust makes two disks because, the way I look at it, if you are going to make piecrust, you may as well make enough for two desserts. It's the same amount of effort and piecrusts freeze really well to use at a later date.

1¼ cups unbleached
all-purpose flour

1 cup whole wheat pastry flour

¼ teaspoon fine sea salt

¾ cup (1½ sticks) unsalted butter

½ cup plain 2 percent Greek yogurt

4 tablespoons ice water

Yogurt Piecrust per disk
Calories 1064
Fat 69 g
Carbs 91 g
Fiber 6 g
Protein 19 g

In the bowl of a food processor fitted with the metal blade, combine the unbleached all-purpose flour, whole wheat pastry flour, and salt, then add the butter. Process until the mixture resembles coarse meal, 8 to 10 seconds.

With the processor on pulse, add the yogurt and enough of the ice water, 1 tablespoon at a time, until the dough holds together without being sticky or crumbly. Halve the dough into 2 equal portions, shape into 2 disks, and wrap each in plastic wrap. Chill until firm and the moisture has distributed evenly, about 30 minutes.

Flour a clean work surface and a rolling pin. (If making a double-crust pie or two pie shells, work with one disk at a time, keeping the second disk chilled.) Place a dough disk in the center of the floured surface. Starting in the center of the dough, roll to, but not over, the upper edge of the dough. Return to the center, and roll down to, but not over, the lower edge. Lift the dough, give it a quarter turn, and lay it on the work surface. Continue rolling, repeating the quarter turns, until you have a disk about ⅛ inch thick.

Ease the pastry into an 11-inch pie plate. Trim 1 inch larger than the diameter of the pie plate; fold the overhanging pastry under itself along the rim of the plate. For a simple decorative edge, press the tines of a fork around the folded pastry. To make a fluted edge, using both your finger and thumb, pinch and crimp the folded dough. Chill until firm, about 30 minutes. Use immediately or freeze for later use.

BLIND BAKING

To blind bake, preheat the oven to 425°F. Crumple a piece of parchment paper, then lay it out flat over the bottom of the pastry. Weight the paper with pie weights, dried beans, or uncooked rice. (This will keep the unfilled piecrust from puffing up in the oven.)

For a partially baked shell that will be filled and baked further, as with Old-Fashioned Buttermilk Pie (page 203), bake for 20 minutes. Remove from the oven and remove the paper and weights. (You can reuse the rice or beans for blind baking a number of times.) The shell can now be filled and baked further, according to the recipe directions.

For a fully baked shell that will hold an uncooked filling, bake the empty shell until a deep golden brown, about 30 minutes total.

STOVETOP APPLE PIE

SERVES 8

There are times in everyone's life when you need something sweet. It's a feeling that won't go away, it's a craving that needs to be sated. It's emergency time and you think if you look at one more blasted tangerine or one more ding-dang frozen grape you are going to scream. I've got your back. This sensible splurge is sweet, crunchy, buttery, and best of all? It's quick. And it's also easy to toss together for company in nonemergency situations.

PIE TOPPING

1 tablespoon unsalted butter

1 teaspoon canola oil

1/2 cup quick oatmeal

3 tablespoons firmly packed light brown sugar

1/4 cup coarsely chopped pecans, hazelnuts, or walnuts

Pinch fine sea salt

APPLE FILLING

1 teaspoon canola oil

4 large apples, such as Granny Smith or Honeycrisp, peeled, cored, and sliced into sixteenths (about 2 pounds)

1 tablespoon granulated sugar

1/2 teaspoon ground cinnamon

1/2 teaspoon ground ginger

1/4 teaspoon ground allspice

1 tablespoon freshly squeezed lemon juice

1 teaspoon pure vanilla extract

Pinch of fine sea salt

Vanilla Cream, for serving (page 197)

Calories 180
Fat 6 g
Carbs 31 g
Fiber 3 g
Protein 3 g

Line a rimmed baking sheet with a nonstick silicone baking mat. (Parchment paper doesn't work as well because the sugar will stick.) To make the topping, heat the butter and oil in a large nonstick skillet over medium heat. Add the oatmeal, brown sugar, nuts, and salt. Cook, stirring constantly, until lightly browned. Transfer to the prepared baking sheet and smooth with an offset spatula into a thin layer. Set aside to cool. Once cooled, crumble into bite-size bits and set aside.

To make the filling, heat the oil in large skillet over medium-high heat. Add the apples and cook, stirring occasionally, until softened, about 5 minutes. Sprinkle with granulated sugar, cinnamon, ginger, and allspice and cook over medium heat, stirring occasionally, until tender, about 5 to 10 minutes. Stir in the lemon juice, vanilla, and a pinch of salt.

To serve, spoon the warm apples into bowls. Top with pie topping and a dollop of vanilla cream. Serve immediately.

CITRUS PUDDING CAKES

SERVES 8

Pudding cakes are the best of both worlds, the ridiculous and wonderful marriage of smooth creamy pudding and the moist, tender, compact crumb of cake. The cake rises to the top and there's a warm, puddinglike sauce below. The key to the success of this dessert is a bain-marie, or water bath. It's used to heat delicate mixtures, often egg-based custards such as this. It creates a gentle, uniform heat around the food—and prevents this pudding cake from becoming a puddle of sweet scrambled eggs.

Other than the bit of fuss with the bain-marie, pudding cakes are a flash to throw together. I particularly like using citrus in desserts. I've used lemon, grapefruit, and orange with this recipe, all with equal success. If you want to chef it up a bit, try adding some chopped fresh herbs. Combinations that really sing are basil with grapefruit and tarragon with orange.

1 cup granulated sugar

$^1/_3$ cup unbleached all-purpose flour

$^1/_8$ teaspoon fine sea salt

1 cup 2 percent milk

Finely grated zest of 1 lemon

$^1/_2$ cup freshly squeezed lemon juice

2 tablespoons unsalted butter, melted

2 large egg yolks

$^1/_2$ teaspoon finely chopped fresh mint

3 large egg whites, at room temperature

Confectioners' sugar, for dusting

Calories 177
Fat 5 g
Carbs 33 g
Fiber .2 g
Protein 2 g

Preheat the oven to 350°F. Spray eight 6-ounce custard cups or ramekins with nonstick cooking spray; place them in a large deep baking dish. Put a pot of water on to boil for the water bath.

Whisk $^3/_4$ cup of the granulated sugar, the flour, and salt in a medium bowl. Make a well in the dry ingredients. Add the milk, lemon zest, lemon juice, butter, egg yolks, and mint. Whisk until smooth.

Beat the egg whites in a mixing bowl with an electric mixer on medium speed until soft peaks form. Gradually add the remaining $^1/_4$ cup granulated sugar and continue beating until stiff and glossy peaks form. Fold the egg whites into the batter. Evenly divide the batter among the prepared ramekins placed in the roasting pan.

Place the roasting pan in the oven and carefully pour in enough boiling water to come almost halfway up the sides of the ramekins. (Seriously, don't skip this step.)

Bake the pudding cakes until golden brown and the cakes have pulled away slightly from the sides of the ramekins, 25 to 30 minutes. Transfer the ramekins to a wire rack to cool for 15 minutes. Dust with confectioners' sugar and serve warm or at room temperature.

CHASING THE CARROT CAKE

MAKES ONE 2-LAYER CAKE TO SERVE 24

Carrot cakes are oil based, and oil-based cakes are easy, which is why they became so popular. It's simply a matter of grating some carrots and measuring out the dry ingredients. There's no creaming of butter and sugar, no egg whites to whip, no sugar syrup for the frosting. It's a glorified quick bread. And it's healthy, right? Big wrong. Remember the oil? More often than not, carrot cakes are a greasy, dense cake laden with frosting and topped with garish exclamations of orange and misshapen squiggles of green. This cake rescues the carrot cake. It still contains oil, but as little as possible and still stays moist.

Yes, you can have cake! Not fake cake, not dry-as-dirt cake—not cake that tastes like it's meant to keep you regular. Real, moist cake. It's still simple to prepare and swathed in a swoopy, winter white coat of sweetened cream cheese frosting, but much lower in calories and fat.

1 (8-ounce) can crushed pineapple in pineapple juice

2¼ cups whole wheat pastry flour, plus more for dusting the pans

1¼ teaspoons baking powder

1 teaspoon baking soda

1 teaspoon fine sea salt

1 teaspoon ground cinnamon

¼ teaspoon ground allspice

¼ teaspoon freshly grated nutmeg

1 cup chopped pecans

½ cup golden raisins

1½ cups granulated sugar

3 large eggs

½ cup canola oil

1 teaspoon pure vanilla extract

3 cups grated carrots (4 to 6 medium)

Preheat the oven to 350°F. Spray two 9-inch round cake pans with nonstick cooking spray. Line with parchment paper. Spray again, and dust with flour. Set aside.

Drain the pineapple in a sieve set over a bowl, pressing on the solids. Reserve the drained pineapple and pineapple juice.

In a large mixing bowl, sift together flour, baking powder, baking soda, salt, cinnamon, allspice, and nutmeg. Add the pecans and raisins, tossing to combine and coat. (This will prevent the nuts and raisins from sinking to the bottom.) Set aside.

In the bowl of a stand mixer fitted with the paddle attachment, combine the sugar and eggs. Beat at low speed until well combined. Add the oil in a slow steady stream, pausing as needed if the mixture starts looking too greasy and unincorporated, until the mixture is smooth. Add the flour-nut mixture, vanilla, and grated carrots. Mix on low speed until combined. Divide the batter evenly between the prepared pans.

Bake until a wooden pick inserted in the center of the layers comes out clean and the sides start to pull away from the edges of pans, 35 to 40 minutes. Let layers cool in the pans for 10 minutes. Remove

CONTINUED

FROSTING

1 (8-ounce) package low-fat cream cheese, at room temperature

1 teaspoon pure vanilla extract

Pinch of fine sea salt

1 pound confectioners' sugar, sifted

Pecan halves, for garnish

Calories 289
Fat 12 g
Carbs 45 g
Fiber 2 g
Protein 3 g

from the pans and place on wire racks, top-side down, to cool completely. Remove the parchment paper. Brush with reserved pineapple juice.

Meanwhile, to make the frosting, in the bowl of a stand mixer fitted with the whisk or paddle attachment, combine the cream cheese, vanilla, and salt. With mixer running on low speed, add the confectioners' sugar. Blend until smooth and consistent. Set the frosting aside, or refrigerate until ready to use.

Once the cake rounds have cooled completely, and when ready to frost, place the first layer on a cake stand or a cardboard cake round, "top" side down. Using a small offset spatula, evenly cover the top of the first layer with about 1 cup of frosting. Spread the frosting so that it extends to the edge of the cake. Place the other cake layer, with the "top" side down, on top of the frosting; press to make it level. With the small offset spatula, spread the top of the cake with the remaining frosting. Garnish around the top with the pecan halves. Slice with a serrated knife and serve. Store in an airtight container in the refrigerator up to 3 days.

PINEAPPLE RIGHT-SIDE-UP CAKE

SERVES 16

Upside-down cake typically has pretty upside-down nutritionals. Not here! Pineapple tossed with brown sugar and dabbed with butter excels as a topping for this pineapple right-side-up cake. No heavy skillets filled with buttery molten lava to flip and risk life and limb, just brown sugar goodness scattered across the top of yielding, tender cake.

Replacing oil or butter with applesauce is a great way to add moisture and flavor to your baking while cutting fat and calories. Typically, it's a one-to-one ratio for most baked goods except cookies, but be aware it can change the texture.

1/2 pineapple, peeled, cored, and diced

2 tablespoons firmly packed dark brown sugar

3/4 cup unbleached all-purpose flour

3/4 cup whole wheat pastry flour

2/3 cup sugar

1 teaspoon baking powder

1/2 teaspoon baking soda

1/4 teaspoon fine sea salt

1 large egg

1 large egg white

2/3 cup low-fat buttermilk

1/3 cup unsweetened applesauce

1 teaspoon pure vanilla extract

1 tablespoon unsalted butter, melted

Calories 114
Fat 2 g
Carbs 22 g
Fiber 1 g
Protein 2 g

Preheat the oven to 350°F. Spray a 9-inch cake pan with nonstick cooking spray. Set aside. In a small bowl combine the pineapple with the brown sugar. Set aside.

In a medium bowl, whisk together the unbleached all-purpose flour, whole wheat pastry flour, sugar, baking powder, baking soda, and sea salt. Add the egg, egg white, buttermilk, applesauce, and vanilla. Whisk to combine. Pour into the prepared pan. Top with the reserved pineapple and drizzle over the melted butter. Transfer to the oven and bake until the sides are pulling from the sides of the pan and the topping is the golden brown, about 45 minutes. Remove to a rack to cool slightly. Cut with a serrated knife and serve warm. Store in an airtight container at room temperature for up to 3 days.

BIG RICH TEXAS SHEET CAKE

SERVES 24

I once heard a joke from one of my cooking class students, a Texan: A teacher was explaining to her geography class about the enormity of the Grand Canyon. Her student Little Johnny was from Texas. He used to brag about how big Texas was, how great Texas was, how strong Texans were, and how Texas was the best state in the entire United States. It wore the teacher, a non-Texan, out. The teacher smiles and says to Little Johnny, "Y'all don't have anything like this in Texas." True to Texas form, Little Johnny smiles wide and says to the teacher, "No ma'am, but we've got enough dirt to fill it." Everything in Texas is big: big hair, big diamonds, and big appetites. Texas Sheet Cake is a moist, tender chocolate cake topped with a chocolate frosting and a sprinkling of pecans. This lightened up version is right on the money.

CAKE

1/4 cup unsweetened cocoa, plus more for dusting the pan

2 cups unbleached all-purpose flour

1 1/2 cups granulated sugar

1 teaspoon baking soda

1/4 teaspoon fine sea salt

3/4 cup water

1/4 cup unsalted butter

1/4 cup canola oil

1/2 cup low-fat buttermilk

1 teaspoon pure vanilla extract

2 large eggs

FROSTING

1/4 cup (1/2 stick) unsalted butter

1/4 cup low-fat buttermilk

1/4 cup unsweetened cocoa

2 cups confectioners' sugar

1 teaspoon pure vanilla extract

1/4 cup chopped pecans, toasted

Preheat the oven to 350°F. Coat a 12 by 17-inch rimmed baking sheet with nonstick cooking spray and dust with cocoa, set aside.

To make the cake, combine the flour, granulated sugar, baking soda, and salt in the bowl of an electric mixer fitted with the paddle attachment. In a small saucepan over medium heat, combine the water, butter, canola oil, and the 1/4 cup cocoa, whisking frequently, until melted and smooth. Add to the flour mixture on medium speed until well blended. Add the buttermilk, vanilla, and eggs; mix well. Pour the batter into the prepared pan. Bake until the center springs back when lightly touched and the sides just start to pull away from the pan, about 13 to 15 minutes. Remove to a wire rack to cool.

To make the frosting, combine the butter, buttermilk, and cocoa in a small saucepan over medium heat, whisking until melted and smooth. Remove from heat. Gradually whisk in the confectioners' sugar and vanilla until smooth. Spread over the warm cake and sprinkle with pecans. Cool completely on wire rack. Slice with a serrated knife and serve. The cake keeps in an airtight container in the refrigerator up to 3 days.

Calories 206
Fat 8 g
Carbs 32 g
Fiber .7 g
Protein 2 g

CHOCOLATE "BROOKIES"

Some folks like desserts like cakes, pies, and cookies, but I'm predominantly a chocolate fan. I like cakes, pies, and cookies, too—but for me, the best desserts are chocolate and the darker the better. Dark chocolate is actually good for you—in moderation. It's the best medical news since they figured out that bloodletting doesn't work. Dark chocolate contains antioxidants and they help protect the body from damage caused by harmful molecules called free radicals that are implicated in heart disease, cancer, and other ailments.

These brownie-cookie mash-ups are rich, intense bursts of concentrated chocolate flavor. They get their out-of-this-world taste from the combination of cocoa powder and bittersweet chocolate. Make sure to look for chocolate with at least 60 percent cacao solids for maximum flavor. In all seriousness, they aren't actually a health food due to the other ingredients, but I guarantee you'll be satisfied when you try one or two of these as a sensible splurge.

1 tablespoon unsalted butter

4 ounces bittersweet chocolate, coarsely chopped

1 cup unbleached all-purpose flour

3/4 cup unsweetened cocoa

1 teaspoon baking powder

1/4 teaspoon fine sea salt

1 1/2 cups sugar

2 large egg whites

2 large eggs

1 tablespoon instant espresso powder, dissolved in 1 tablespoon hot water

1 teaspoon vanilla extract

Calories 69
Fat 2 g
Carbs 13 g
Fiber .4 g
Protein 1 g

Preheat the oven to 350°F. Line a rimmed baking sheet with a non-stick silicone mat or parchment paper.

Place the butter and chocolate in a microwave-safe bowl; microwave on high power 30 seconds and stir. Repeat the process in 10 second intervals until the ingredients are melted and smooth. Set aside.

Whisk together the flour, cocoa, baking powder, and salt in a medium bowl, and set aside. In the bowl of an electric mixer fitted with the paddle attachment, combine the sugar, egg whites, and eggs on medium speed until thick and pale, about 5 minutes. Decrease the speed to low and add the reserved chocolate mixture, espresso, and vanilla. Gradually add the flour mixture until just combined.

Drop the dough by rounded tablespoonfuls 2 inches apart on the prepared baking sheet. Bake until just set and the tops just begin to crack, about 10 minutes. Remove to a rack to cool slightly then remove with a metal spatula to the rack cool completely. Store in an airtight container for up to 1 week.

CLAIRE'S CREAM CHEESE SWIRL BROWNIES

MAKES 16 2-INCH SQUARE BROWNIES

These are what I like to call "grown woman" brownies. These are not PTA bake sale brownies. These are dark, rich, knock-your-socks-off chocolate brownies. I was actually bribed for this recipe before the publication of this cookbook. How'd I do it? I have a friend Claire Perez, a French-trained pastry chef, to thank. It may seem counterintuitive to seek assistance from a chef who worked with the master chefs of butter and confection, Jacques Torres and Pierre Hermé, for a "lightened up" brownie recipe. But Claire delivered the goods!

4 ounces reduced-fat cream cheese

1 cup plus 2 tablespoons sugar

1/2 teaspoon pure vanilla extract

2 large eggs, at room temperature

3/4 cup whole wheat pastry flour

1/2 cup cocoa powder

3/4 teaspoon baking powder

1/2 teaspoon fine sea salt

1/4 cup canola oil

6 ounces best-quality semisweet chocolate, finely chopped

1 cup sugar

1/2 cup low-fat buttermilk

1/2 cup unsweetened applesauce

2 teaspoons pure vanilla extract

Calories 199
Fat 9 g
Carbs 27 g
Fiber 2 g
Protein 3 g

Preheat the oven to 325°F. Spray an 8-inch square baking pan with nonstick cooking spray.

In the bowl of an electric mixer fitted with the paddle attachment, combine the cream cheese, the 2 tablespoons of sugar, and vanilla, stirring until creamy and smooth. Separate one of the eggs, reserving the white for later use, and add the yolk to the cream cheese mixture. Stir to combine, then set aside.

In a small bowl, whisk together the flour, cocoa, baking powder, and salt; set aside.

In a medium saucepan, heat the oil and chocolate over medium heat, whisking until the chocolate is melted. Whisk in the sugar and stir until melted. Add the buttermilk, applesauce, and vanilla. Remove from the heat. Add the remaining whole egg and the reserved egg white, whisking constantly until incorporated to prevent the eggs from curdling. Add the reserved flour mixture, mixing until just combined. Transfer brownie batter to the prepared pan.

Using a tablespoon, drop 9 dollops of the cream cheese mixture on top of the brownie batter. Draw the tip of a sharp knife or skewer through the two batters in a criss-cross fashion to create a swirled effect.

Bake the brownies until the top is just firm to the touch, rotating halfway through baking, about 40 minutes. Let cool completely in the pan on a wire rack.

Coat a serrated knife with nonstick cooking spray and cut into 16 squares. Store in an airtight container in the refrigerator up to 3 days.

Acknowledgments

FIRST, I WANT TO THANK my sister Jona Willis, who endured daily texts every time I got off the scales with a victory. Your faith in me is endless and I am most grateful. I love you.

I wouldn't be the cook or person I am without the love and caring of my sweet Mama. Thank you for teaching me the joys of the kitchen and being one of the best friends I could ever have.

To have "met your match" often means someone is better than you and will beat you at the task at hand. At least that is what I thought until I actually met my match. Then, I realized that "meeting your match" is better described as finding the other piece of your own personal puzzle. Thank you Lisa, for being the fast to my slow, the unedited to my edited, the North to my South, and the piece that makes me feel complete.

Renaissance woman Angie Mosier is a photographer, stylist, baker, cook, writer, artist, and producer. She's also clever, funny, and lovely—an all-around awesome woman. I appreciate her friendship and thank her for her work.

Claire Perez and her smart and beautiful daughter Ruby Funfrock are my supporters, my friends, and chosen family. I am so grateful to have Claire at my side in the baker's kitchen and as one of my dearest friends. Ruby, you continue to astonish and amaze me; I hope to continue cooking with both of you for years to come.

Many thanks to my mentors Nathalie Dupree and Anne Willan as well as a long list of friends, testers, helpers, and eaters: Sandy and Angie D'Amato, Gena Berry, Evan Bernstein and Rich Wilner, Regina Beyer, Jenni Coale, Tamie Cook, Holly Chute, Elise Garner, Lizzie Johnston, Rebecca Lang, Debi Loftis, John Mata, Barbara Owens, and Barb Pires. Thanks to Anne Cain for working with me to ensure the recipes tasted great and still hit good nutritional marks.

I have long been a partner with Whole Foods Market and appreciate the kind support of Cheryl Galway and Darrah Horgan. Thanks to Katie Cash Hayes and the Community Farmers' Markets, especially the Grant Park Farmers' Market. Big shout out to The Cooks Warehouse with Mary Moore and her stellar team, including PR guru Jim Brams. Much obliged to Sue Anne Morgan and Sondra Landrum of IdeaLand and Pixie Wizard Graphics for their professionalism, patience, and belief in me. Thanks to Enterprise Farms in South Deerfield, Massachusetts, and Sheila Bowman at Seafood Watch.

Thanks to my editor Emily Timberlake and the great folks at Ten Speed, including Kristin Casemore, Katy Brown, Kara Plikaitis, Anitra Alcantara, and Lorraine Woodcheke, for their great partnership and enabling me to share my work.

The folks at Lisa Ekus Group—Lisa Ekus, Jaimee Constantine, Sally Ekus, Samantha Marsh, Corinne Fay, and Sean Kimball—are the best cheerleaders ever. I am thankful to be a part of their talented group of authors and clients.

Index

Library of Congress Cataloging-in-Publication Data

Willis, Virginia, 1966-

Lighten up, y'all : classic Southern recipes made healthy and
wholesome / Virginia Willis.

pages cm

1. Cooking, American—Southern style. 2. Low-fat diet—Recipes.
I. Title.

TX715.2.S68W5563 2015

641.5975—dc23

Hardcover ISBN: 978-1-60774-573-0

eBook ISBN: 978-1-60774-574-7

Printed in China

Design by Katy Brown

10 9 8 7 6 5 4 3 2 1

First Edition

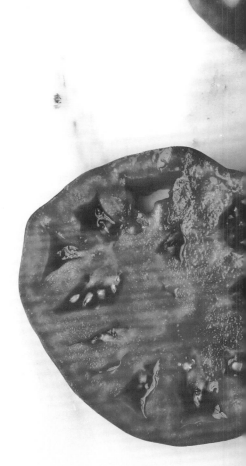